250 Authentic Recipes from 111 Countries

THE COOKBOOK OF THE UNITED NATIONS

Compiled and Edited by
Barbara Kraus

Published by the
United Nations Association of the United States of America, Inc.

United Nations Association of the United States of America, Inc. is the result of a merger between the United States Committee for the United Nations and the American Association for the United Nations. This non-partisan, non-profit organization is composed of individual members active in local chapters throughout the country, and major national organizations. Its purpose is to disseminate facts about and arouse interest in the United Nations through informational and educational programs.

Printed in the U. S. A.
Library of Congress Catalog Card Number: 64-21341

Foreword

Here is a completely new collection of authentic, interesting, and delicious recipes from the countries of the United Nations.

The Cookbook of the United Nations represents a four-year labor of love by hundreds of generous friends of the United Nations throughout the world who tracked down and perfected the culinary specialties in this book. Authorship rightfully belongs to representatives and/or their wives of the diplomatic corps, members of the international Secretariat of the UN, by American citizens who treasure their parents' native dishes, and by many other gourmets. To all of them, we express our deep gratitude.

Mildred Horton, the American member of the Executive Committee of the International Federation of Home Economics, contributed invaluable assistance both editorially and in reviewing the avalanche of recipes for final selection. From over 750 suggestions we chose those recipes that seemed most unusual and which could easily be converted to authentic dishes for the American kitchen.

Each recipe was tested and retested professionally by home economists in their own homes for their own families, and frequently for guests from the country of origin. This international "judging" insured consistently correct standards for ingredients, procedure and results.

The Cookbook of the United Nations provides both information and inspiration for those planning international menus for United Nations Day, October 24 — a growing tradition here and abroad.

Barbara Kraus

October 24, 1964

Acknowledgments

We wish to thank the following individuals who have contributed recipes, the home economists who have tested them, and the test kitchens of corporations who have converted some of these to large-scale.

Readers of this cookbook may wish to contribute recipes for Volume II . . . if so, please contact the editor.

Contributors of Recipes Mrs. Paul Abernathy, Mme. Diop Alassane, Mrs. Ahmed Mouwahid Aly, Mrs. Rivka Angel, Mr. Nessim Arditi, Mrs. Simone Attwood, Mrs. Tillie Avrami, Mr. André O. Backar, Miss Norma Bandak, Bangor Overseas Women's Club, H. E. Mr. James Barrington, Miss Rosa Bejar, Mrs. Jean K. Benjamin, Mr. C. F. N. Bentley, H. E. M. Armand Bérard, M. Maurice Bertrand, Mrs. Judith Bingham, Mrs. Lee Blackwell, Mr. Vadim Bogoslovsky, Mrs. Betty Boyd, Sra. Dora B. de Boyd, Mr. S. A. Bronnikov, Sra. Corina de Caballero Tamayo, M. Caimerom Measketh

Hon. John A. Calhoun, Mr. Thomas A. Cassily, Sra. Graciela Ponce de Leon de Cattarossi, Chef Maxime Chalmin, Miss Grace Chen, Commander Harry Archer Clark, U. S. N. (Ret.), Mme. Odette Cohen, H. E. M. Sori Coulibaly, Sra. Ana H. de Cuevas, Miss Marie José Damas, Mr. Robert de Vaughn, Patricia W. Dean, H. E. Dr. Francisco A. Delgado, Mme. John Dubé, Princess Dumbadze, Mr. William L. Eagleton, Jr., Miss Selma Ekrem, Mrs. Nermin El Masri, H. E. Mr. Hassan Nur Elmi, Mrs. Marjorie P. Essien, Miss Joan Evanish, Mrs. Afaf Fahmy, Dr. A. G. Ravan Farhadi, H. E. Mr. B. G. Fourie, Sylvia Howard Fuhrman, H. E. Sr. Alfonso Garcia-Robles, H. E. Dr. Vasco Vieira Garin, Mme. Régine Gbedey, Mr. Ignacij Golob, Mrs. Estelle Grad, Miss Maureen Adikes Grenier

Mr. Alfonso Grez, H. E. M. Georges Hakim, Miss Grace Halsell, Mrs. J. G. H. Halstead, Mr. Kurt Hampe, Mr. Mario C. J. Harrington, Miss Rozina Hirji, Mrs. Hans Hoffmann, Mr. Charles A. Hogan, Mme. Louis Ignacio-Pinto, M. Ernest M. Jean-Louis, Mr. Keith Johnson, Miss Charlotte Kahler, H. E. Mr. Philip M. Kaiser, Mr. Frank P. Karefa-Smart, Mr. Joseph Kazigo, Mrs. O. H. Kelfa-Caulker, H. E. Mr. Eamonn L. Kennedy, Mrs. John F. Kennedy, Mr. Tibor Keszthelyi, Dr. Flemmie P. Kittrell, Mrs. Vanda Kreacic, H. E. Mr. Karel Kurka

M. Jules Laventure, Mr. Alphonse Lema, H. E. Mr. Bohdan Lewandowski, Miss Mette Lie, Mrs. Teow-Chong Lim, Mr. Harry Lindquist, Dr. Chang S. Liu, Berenice MacFarquhar, Mr. W. McIlquham Schmidt, Mrs. Gunapala Piyasena Malalasekera, H. E. M. Ackhar Marof, H. E. Srta. Carmen Natalia Martinez Bonilla, Mrs. Betti Richard Matsch, H. E. Dr. Koto Matsudaira, Miss Marie Lee McBroom, Mrs. Mildred Mehl, Mrs. Thomas P. Melady, H. E. Mr. Turgut Menemencioglu, Miss Anne Michaels, Mr. Waclaw Micuta, Miss Tonia Moffat

Miss Magdalena W. Muya, Mr. E. U. Oton, Mrs. Julian V. Pace, M. Tiao Phouangsavath, Sra. Luz B. de Pinies, Sra. Clara de Ponce de Leon, Sr. Raúl Quijano, Mrs. Marta C. Raymond, Mrs. Beatrice Reachelson, Mr. M. Jusuf Ronodipuro, Mrs.David Rosen, Mrs. Teresa Rossides, Mrs. Samuel Rubin, Mr. Federico Rufe, Miss Najwa Sarkis, Mr. Serafim Serafimov, H. E. Mr. Rishikesh Shaha, Mrs. Basima Saeed Shammas, Mr. R. W. Sharp, Mrs. Jacq Siracusa, Mr. A. R. Sitnikov, Mrs. Emilia A. Sley, Miss Elizabeth Smith, Mrs. Sheilah Solomon

Mrs. Alkione Stathakos, H. E. Mr. Adlai E. Stevenson, Mrs. El Nur Ali Suleiman, Mrs. Marie Syrovy, Mrs. Najiba Tabibi, Mr. M. A. K. Taha, Mme. Jacqueline Tapsoba, Miss Mollie Thompson, Mrs. Thor Thors, Mrs. Elizabeth Ticknor, Mrs. Franca Tolbert, M. Robert Treboux, Hon. Marietta P. Tree, Sra. Marta Yolanda de Trigueros, H. E. Sr. Vincente Urcuyo Rodriguez, Mrs. Homa Vakil, Mrs. Jitinder Valhali, Mr. J. P. A. M. van den Bogaert, Mr. Carlos S. Vegega, Miss Constance Venable, Mrs. Fernando Volio, Miss Agatha Wangeci, Mr. D. Weahplah Wilson, Mme. Junie Woulbroun-Bovesse, Miss Ophelia Yuén, Mrs. Guri Lie Zeckendorf

Home Economists Mrs. John Bang, Dr. A. June Bricker (Executive Director of the American Home Economics Association), Mrs. Gerald L. Brower, Mrs. Sybil Butleman, Mrs. Selma H. Cohen, Mrs. Robert Conway, Mrs. Eula Bee Corban, Mrs. Robert Deal, Mrs. R. C. Diehl, Jr., Mrs. Ruth Dougherty, Miss Belle Dubin, Mrs. Alma C. DuMont, Mrs. Barbara Erickson, Mrs. Fred C. Francis, Mrs. A. H. Fricke, Jr., Mrs. Marjorie Fritzsche, Mrs. Elaine Gaines, Mrs. Shirley Heit, Mrs. John N. Herron, Miss Mildred Horton

Mrs. I. Reid Howland, Mrs. William Imershein, Mrs. Dorothy S. Jackson, Mrs. Charlotte V. Jacobson, Mrs. Dorothy L. Jefferson, Mrs. A. C. Jenkins, Mrs. Ruth Johnson, Mrs. Carolyn Jones, Mrs. Martin Koenig, Mrs. Janet Koral, Mrs. Eileen Lambert, Mrs. Helene Landau, Mrs. Lillian Lester, Mrs. Selma Lieberman, Mrs. Emily E. Mattox, Mrs. E. A. Mueller, Mrs. Barbara Murphy, Mrs. Travis Nelson, Mrs. John L. O'Brien, Mrs. Edith Ordan, Mrs. J. Donald Osborne, Miss Ruth E. Ostrander, Mrs. Ann Ritterman

Mrs. Charles J. Roesch, Mrs. Carol P. Romberg, Mrs. Barbara Romero, Mrs. Marjorie Schrier, Mrs. Helen K. Schwartz, Mrs. Earl Slade, Mrs. W. C. Sloan, Mrs. Robert Soost, Mrs. Eleanor Werner, Mrs. Margaret E. Whitbeck, Mrs. S. H. White, Mrs. Mildred Winston, Mrs. Katherine Woodhouse, Mrs. Robert H. Young, Mrs. Millicent Zarr

Test Kitchens Home Service Department of Best Foods, Division of Corn Products Co.; Kellogg Company; The Kraft Kitchens; The Lipton Kitchens; NABISCO; The Pillsbury Company; Sealtest Foods Consumer Service; Theodore R. Sills and Co.; and Standard Brands Incorporated.

CONTENTS

AFGHANISTAN

Ashaks (Leek Ravioli)

Ashaks

3 cups flour
1½ teaspoons salt
1 cup water

Filling:

20 stalks tender leeks
2 tablespoons melted margarine
½ teaspoon salt
⅛ teaspoon pepper

Sour Cream Mixture:

1 pint sour cream
¼ teaspoon garlic powder (or to taste)
½ teaspoon salt

Meat Sauce:

2 cups chopped onions
½ cup melted margarine
1 pound ground beef
1 teaspoon salt
½ teaspoon pepper
2 tablespoons tomato sauce
1 cup water
2 tablespoons chopped mint

Combine flour and salt in a mixing bowl; add ½ cup water and mix with a fork. Add remaining water, 2 tablespoons at a time until the dough is of right consistency to roll. Turn out on floured board and knead lightly. Cover and allow to stand for 15 minutes. Divide dough into fourths. Roll out each fourth very thin; cut into circles with a 3-inch cookie cutter.

To make filling: clean leeks and remove any discolored leaves. Chop entire leek very fine. Add melted margarine, salt, and pepper.

Put 2 teaspoons of leek filling on lower half of each circle. Moisten edges of top half with water; fold top half over and seal edges with tines of a fork. Place on a lightly floured plate, at least an inch apart to prevent their sticking together. Drop filled circles or Ashaks into a large pot, ¾ filled with rapidly boiling water. Boil for 5 minutes (count time after water returns to boiling). Remove Ashaks from water with slotted spoon.

To make sour cream mixture: combine sour cream, garlic powder, and salt. Place Ashaks on a platter over which a thin layer of sour cream mixture has been spread; cover Ashaks with remaining sour cream mixture.

To make meat sauce: cook onions in fat until lightly browned; add remaining ingredients, except the water and mint. Cook over low heat until meat loses its pinkish color. Add water and cook slowly until water evaporates. Spoon meat sauce over the top of the Ashaks and sprinkle with chopped mint. Yield: 6 to 8 servings.

Kabeli Pilau (Chicken and Rice)

- 1 4-pound stewing chicken, cut in pieces
- 2 large onions, sliced
- 2 teaspoons salt
- 8 cups hot water
- 1 cup long grain rice
- 1 cup thinly sliced onions
- 2 tablespoons butter
- 1 teaspoon ground cardamon
- 1 teaspoon ground cumin
- 3 carrots, cooked and sliced
- ½ cup raisins, seedless

Place chicken pieces, onions, salt, and hot water in a 3-quart sauce pan or kettle. Simmer for 2½ to 3 hours; chicken should be tender, yet firm. Remove and cool chicken; save broth; remove meat from bone; use only large pieces for this dish. Cook rice according to directions on package. When done, keep covered until used.

To make broth sauce, brown onions in hot butter; remove from heat; add cardamon and cumin; mash with onion to form a paste. Add 2½ cups of the chicken broth; simmer for 5 minutes; taste for seasonings.

Combine cooked rice, broth sauce, and chicken; put in buttered casserole; place carrots on top of mixture; sprinkle raisins on top of carrots. Cover; cook in a 325°F oven for 35 to 45 minutes. Add broth or water if dish is dry. When done, mix carrots and raisins lightly with chicken and rice. Broth not used in main dish can be served as soup course. Yield: 6-8 servings.

ALBANIA

Kabuni (Rice and Raisin Dessert)

- ¼ pound butter or margarine
- 2 cups boiling water
- 1 cup long-grain rice
- 1 cup raisins, washed
- ½ cup sugar
- 2½ teaspoons cinnamon

Add butter or margarine to boiling water; when fat is melted, add rice and raisins. Let rice mixture come to a boil; reduce to simmering. Cover; cook rice until liquid is absorbed and rice is tender.

Sprinkle bottom of deep serving dish with 2 tablespoons of sugar and ½ teaspoon of cinammon; cover with a layer of rice, using about ¼ of the rice. Repeat layers making a total of 4. Sprinkle remaining ½ teaspoon of cinnamon on top layer of rice. Serve warm as dessert with sweet cream or ice cream. Yield: 6-8 servings.

Note: The amount of butter or margarine may be reduced or even omitted completely with good results.

Pul Me Harr (Chicken with Walnuts)

- 1 3½ to 5-pound hen
- 1 teaspoon salt
- ½ teaspoon pepper
- 2 cups water
- 1 pound shelled walnuts
- 4 tablespoons butter
- 2 tablespoons flour
- ½ to 1 teaspoon garlic powder

Season hen with salt and pepper. Place hen in large baking pan with cover; add 2 cups of water. Cover; cook chicken in 325°F oven for 2 hours or until chicken is tender. When chicken is done, remove from pan and cut into serving pieces. Save broth.

To make sauce, crush walnuts in a blender or with a rolling pin. Melt butter in a 12-inch skillet over low heat; stir in flour, continuing to stir until flour is brown. Add the crushed walnuts, garlic powder, and gradually 2 cups of the chicken broth to the browned mixture. Blend the ingredients; add chicken to the sauce, coating each piece with the sauce; continue cooking over low heat until sauce is thick. Remove from heat; cover and let stand 5 to 10 minutes before serving. Yield: 6 servings.

ALGERIA

Algerian Meat Balls

- 2 slices dry bread
- ½ cup milk
- 1 pound ground beef or lamb
- ½ cup finely chopped onion
- ½ teaspoon dried dill weed
- ½ cup chopped fresh parsley or ¼ cup dried parsley
- ½ teaspoon dried mint leaves
- 1 egg, slightly beaten
- ¾ teaspoon salt
- ¼ teaspoon pepper
- Oil or fat for deep-fat frying

Soak bread in milk until soft; squeeze out excess milk. To the bread, add all ingredients listed, except fat for frying. Mix all ingredients very thoroughly; if too thick to shape easily, add milk in which the bread was soaked. Roll mixture into 1-inch balls. Fry a few at a time in deep fat at 370°F until balls are golden brown. Remove from fat, drain, and serve. Yield: 18-24 appetizers.

Chakchouka (Mixed Vegetables with Eggs)

4 large onions, sliced
3 tablespoons oil
4 large tomatoes; peeled and sliced
3 large sweet green peppers, chopped
1 small hot pepper, chopped
1 tablespoon vinegar
1½ teaspoons salt
6 eggs
1 green pepper, grilled, skinned, and cut in thin strips

Cook onions in oil in a 10-inch frying pan until golden brown; add all of the ingredients except the eggs and pepper strips. Simmer until the vegetables are reduced to a pulp.

Make 6 indentations in the vegetables and carefully break an egg into each one. Cover the frying pan and cook over low heat until eggs are well set. Garnish each serving with the strips of green pepper. (Eggs could be beaten with 6 tablespoons of milk, poured over the vegetables, covered, and cooked until set.) Yield: 6 servings.

ARGENTINA

Carbonada Criolla (Beef Stew in Pumpkin Shell)

3 cloves garlic, quartered
3 tablespoons fat
2 large onions, chopped
2 large tomatoes, chopped
1 large green pepper, chopped
2 pounds tender beef, cut in 1-inch cubes
1½ teaspoon salt
½ teaspoon pepper
1 teaspoon sugar
8 dried peach halves
3 medium-size white potatoes, pared and diced
3 small sweet potatoes, pared and diced
2 packages frozen corn, whole kernel
2 cups beef broth or consommé
½ cup Madeira wine

1 medium pumpkin
1 tablespoon melted butter
½ teaspoon salt

Brown garlic in fat; remove and discard. Cook onion in remaining fat until yellow. Add tomatoes, green pepper, beef, salt, pepper, and sugar. Mix thoroughly and simmer for 20 minutes, stirring occasionally. Add peaches, potatoes, corn and broth to meat mixture. Cover; simmer for 40 minutes. (Add more broth during cooking if needed.) Add wine.

Cut top from pumpkin and save. Remove seeds and membranes. Coat inside of pumpkin with butter and salt. Pour stew into pumpkin shell. Replace pumpkin top. Place filled pumpkin on shallow baking pan and bake in a 325°F oven until pumpkin meat is tender. Place pumpkin on bed of green leaves for serving. Yield: 6 servings.

Sopa de Manzanas (Apple Sauce)

- 4 green apples, cut in eighths
- Water
- 4 slices of lemon peel
- ½ cup sugar
- ¼ cup raisins, soaked in warm water
- 1 egg yolk, slightly beaten

Cover apples with cold water, add lemon peel, and cook quickly for 20 to 30 minutes, or until apples are soft. Put the cooked apples through a strainer or food mill to separate sauce from peel and core. Add sugar and raisins. Whip egg yolk into sauce to make it fluffy. Serve warm or cold. Yield: 6 servings.

Lengua con Almendras (Tongue with Almond Sauce)

- 1 tongue, cooked, sliced in thin strips

Sauce:

- 1 clove garlic
- 1 tablespoon olive oil
- 1 small tomato, chopped
- 1½ tablespoons chopped green olives
- 12 almonds, ground
- 1 bay leaf, chopped finely
- ½ teaspoon minced parsley
- 1 cup tongue broth
- 2 to 4 tablespoons sifted bread crumbs

To make sauce: cook garlic in oil and remove when brown. Add other ingredients to the remaining oil, except bread crumbs, and simmer for 10 minutes. Thicken cooked sauce with bread crumbs. Place tongue on top of sauce in large frying pan and heat. Serve with border of parsley-buttered potatoes. Yield: 6 servings.

Beth's Pollo con Limón (Chicken with Lemon)

- 1 2½-pound frying chicken, cut for frying
- 3 tablespoons butter, melted
- 6 tablespoons lemon juice

Sauce:

- 1 cup diced celery
- ¼ cup water
- 3 tablespoons butter
- 3 tablespoons flour
- 2 cups milk
- ½ teaspoon salt
- ¼ teaspoon pepper
- 1 tablespoon sugar
- 2 teaspoons prepared mustard
- ½ teaspoon cider vinegar

Place chicken pieces in a 3-quart casserole; mix butter and lemon juice and pour over chicken. Cover; bake in a 325°F oven for 1 hour or until chicken is done.

To make sauce: cook celery and water in a covered casserole for about 30 minutes in oven while chicken is cooking. Mix melted butter and flour in sauce pan; stir until smooth. Add 1 cup milk gradually; cook over low heat until thick, stirring constantly; add salt and pepper. To the other cup of milk, stir in the sugar and mustard; add vinegar until mixture thickens slightly but without making heavy curds. Combine the two milk mixtures; add the celery and the juices from the cooked chicken and from the celery. Pour sauce over cooked chicken. Yield: 6 servings.

Niños Envueltos (Meat Rolls)

2 pounds sirloin or top round steak, cut ½-inch thick

Marinade:

¾ cup white wine or cider vinegar
2 tablespoons chopped green pepper
1 teaspoon salt
1 teaspoon dry mustard
1 teaspoon sugar
½ clove garlic, minced

Stuffing:

6 slices stale bread, cubed
¾ cup milk
2 eggs, beaten slightly
1 tablespoon chopped parsley
½ teaspoon salt
½ teaspoon pepper
1 tablespoon butter, melted

3 tablespoons fat

Sauce:

1 clove garlic, minced
1 medium onion, minced
3 tablespoons olive oil
1 1-pound can tomatoes
1 tablespoon chopped parsley
3 tablespoons chopped green pepper
½ teaspoon salt
½ teaspoon pepper
½ cup white wine

3 medium potatoes, cut in fourths
1 package frozen peas

Pound steak with meat hammer or the edge of a heavy saucer until meat is thin. Cut in 6 equal strips.

To make marinade: combine all marinade ingredients, simmer for 10 minutes and cool. Pour cooled marinade over meat and let stand 2 to 3 hours. Remove meat from marinade.

To make stuffing: soak bread cubes in milk until soft. Squeeze out excess milk. Combine all ingredients and mix well.

Place an equal portion of stuffing on each of the 6 strips. Roll tightly and secure with string. Brown rolls lightly in fat and place side by side in shallow casserole or baking dish.

To make sauce: cook garlic and onion in oil until yellow. Add other ingredients and simmer for 20 minutes.

Pour sauce over meat rolls and bake covered for 1½ hours in a 325°F oven. Add potatoes after the meat has cooked for 1 hour; add peas 15 minutes later, and continue cooking for 15 minutes. Yield: 6 servings.

AUSTRALIA

Green Pepper Cocktail

- 3 large green peppers, chilled
- 6 tablespoons cold flaked seafood
- 6 tablespoons diced celery
- 6 tablespoons diced cucumbers
- 6 teaspoons lemon juice
- 6 tablespoons mayonnaise
- ½ teaspoon salt
- Few grains cayenne pepper
- Paprika
- 6 lemon wedges

Cut each pepper in half lengthwise; remove seeds. Combine fish, celery, cucumbers, lemon juice, mayonnaise, salt, and pepper. Fill pepper halves with mixture; sprinkle with paprika and serve with lemon wedges. Serve as appetizer or as entrée. Yield: 6 servings.

Caramel Pavlova

- 3 egg whites
- ¾ cup sugar, sifted
- 1 teaspoon grated lemon rind, fresh
- 1 teaspoon vanilla
- ¼ cup chopped nuts

Caramel Filling:

- 1 cup brown sugar
- 2 tablespoons flour
- 2 tablespoons margarine or butter
- 2 egg yolks
- 1 cup milk
- ½ teaspoon vanilla

Beat egg whites in a bowl over hot water until stiff; gradually add 1 teaspoon of sugar at a time; continue beating for 5 minutes or until mixture stands in peaks. Fold in rind and vanilla. Turn on a greased paper on a cooky sheet; shape into a circle the size of a dinner plate; hollow the center and build up the sides to hold filling. Bake in a 250°F oven for 1½ hours or until meringue is crisp and dry. Cool.

To make filling: add sugar and flour to melted butter in medium saucepan; cook over low heat for about 4 minutes, stirring constantly. Beat the egg yolks and milk together; add to first mixture; cook until thick, stirring continuously. Cool; fold in vanilla.

Pour filling into center of cold meringue and sprinkle top with nuts. Serve as dessert. Yield: 6 servings.

Baked Fillets of Whiting

Oil
½ cup grated cheese
1½ pounds fillet of whiting or similar fish
½ teaspoon salt
¼ teaspoon pepper
4 tablespoons chopped shallots or green onions
½ pound fresh mushrooms or 1 4½-ounce can
6 tablespoons white wine
1½ teaspoons lemon juice
1 tablespoon chopped parsley

Oil shallow baking dish; sprinkle with grated cheese. Place fish fillets on cheese; add salt, pepper, and shallots or onions. Top with mushrooms; pour white wine over fillets. Bake in 450°F oven for 15 minutes. Sprinkle with lemon juice and parsley before serving. Yield: 6 servings.

Spiced Steak with Carrot Whirls

1½ pounds top round or chuck beef steak, cut in individual pieces
2 tablespoons flour
1 teaspoon salt
1 teaspoon sugar
½ teaspoon nutmeg
Few grains cayènne pepper
1½ cups meat stock
1 tablespoon tomato sauce
1 tablespoon vinegar
1 onion, sliced

Carrot Whirls:

1 cup flour
1½ teaspoons baking powder
½ teaspoon salt
4 tablespoons shortening
4 tablespoons milk
½ cup grated carrot
1 tablespoon finely diced onion
3 gherkins, chopped
1 tablespoon finely diced parsley

Dredge steak with mixture of flour, salt, sugar, nutmeg, and pepper; place meat in a greased casserole of 2-quart capacity. Mix the stock, tomato sauce, and vinegar together; add to meat; top meat with onion. Cover casserole and cook in 350°F oven for 1 hour.

To make carrot whirls: Sift flour, baking powder, and salt into a mixing bowl; add shortening and blend with flour mixture; add milk to make a fairly soft dough. Knead lightly on a floured board; roll to a rectangular sheet about ¼ inch thick. Spread on sheet of dough the carrot, onion, and gherkins; sprinkle with parsley. Moisten edges with water; roll dough, starting with long side. Chill; cut roll into ½ inch slices.

Place sliced carrot whirls on hot meat mixture; do not cover. Cook in 400°F oven for 15 to 20 minutes or until whirls are puffed and browned. Yield: 6 servings.

AUSTRIA

Tyrolese Soup (Split Pea Soup)

- ½ cup split peas
- 4 cups water
- 1 teaspoon salt
- 2 tablespoons butter or bacon fat
- ¼ cup diced celery
- 1 large potato, diced
- 1 large onion, sliced
- 1 tablespoon chopped parsley
- 1 tablespoon flour

Cook peas, water, and salt until peas are soft; sieve peas and return to water. In separate pan, melt fat; add celery, potato, onion, and parsley; cook until vegetables are tender. Stir flour into fat and vegetable mixture.

Combine the two mixtures; simmer for 15 minutes. Yield: 6 servings.

Salzburger Nockerln (Angel Fluff)

- 2 cups milk, scalded
- 1 tablespoon butter
- 3 egg whites
- 6 tablespoons sugar
- 3 egg yolks
- ½ cup flour
- 1 piece vanilla bean
- ½ cup confectioners sugar

Vanilla Sauce:

- 1½ cups of the milk used for cooking fluffs
- ¼ cup sugar
- 2 egg yolks, beaten
- ½ teaspoon vanilla

Combine milk and butter; pour into a shallow casserole and place in a 350°F oven. Beat eggs whites until frothy; gradually add sugar and beat until stiff. Beat egg yolks until light; add flour to yolks; fold this mixture into egg whites and sugar mixture. Drop mixture by tablespoon into the hot milk; cover casserole and cook in oven for 8 minutes. Remove casserole cover and bake for 6 minutes. Remove nockerlns with slotted spoon; sprinkle with vanilla sugar. (Split a piece of vanilla bean and scrape out the little seeds with a small knife. Combine with confectioners sugar and crush together well.)

To make the sauce: combine milk, sugar and egg yolks; cook over low heat or in a double boiler until custard coats a spoon. Strain and add vanilla.

Pour hot vanilla sauce over nockerlns and serve as dessert. Yield: 6 servings.

Gefuellter Kalbsbraten (Veal Rolls)

7 veal cube steaks
1 medium onion
2 slices bacon
2 tablespoons capers
2 anchovies
½ teaspoon salt
¼ teaspoon pepper
6 hard-cooked eggs
3 tablespoons butter

Grind together one of the veal steaks, onion, bacon, capers, and anchovies; mix well. Sprinkle salt and pepper over the remaining steaks; spread the ground mixture on steaks. Roll each steak around 1 hard-cooked egg, and secure roll with string. Pan-fry in butter until brown and well done. Serve hot as rolls or serve cold cut in slices. Yield: 6 servings.

BELGIUM

Ham and Endive au Gratin

12 stalks endive
½ teaspoon salt
1 cup water
12 small slices cooked ham
4 tablespoons flour
3 tablespoons butter
1 cup water from endives and light cream
1 cup milk
¼ pound Swiss cheese, grated
1 egg, beaten
⅛ teaspoon nutmeg
¼ teaspoon salt
Few grains pepper
1 cup bread crumbs
3 tablespoons melted butter

Simmer cleaned stalks in salted water for 10 minutes. Drain; save liquid. Roll each endive stalk in slice of ham; place in a flat baking dish with edge of ham on dish.

Combine flour and melted butter in frying pan. Add sufficient cream to endive liquid to make 1 cup; add with milk to flour and butter mixture; stir and cook over low heat. Add cheese (reserve ⅓ cup), egg, nutmeg, salt, and pepper. Stir until cheese is melted.

Pour sauce over ham and endive rolls. Combine bread crumbs, melted butter and ⅓ cup cheese; sprinkle over sauce. Bake in 400°F oven for 30 minutes. Yield: 6 servings.

Pâté à la Flamande (Flemish Liver Pâté)

- 1/3 pound sliced bacon, cut into 1-inch lengths
- 3/4 pound pork liver
- 1 bay leaf
- 1/2 teaspoon dried thyme
- 2 tablespoons chopped onion
- 1/2 clove garlic, crushed
- 1 1/2 teaspoons brandy or brandy extract
- 1/4 teaspoon salt
- 1/8 teaspoon pepper
- 2 slices fat pork, 1/4-inch thick

Place bacon, liver, bay leaf, thyme, onion, and garlic in heavy skillet and cook over low heat for 1 hour. Do not drain. Grind this mixture twice through the finest blade of food chopper or blend to a smooth paste in electric blender. Mixture should be free of lumps, strained if necessary. Add brandy, salt, and pepper to paste. Put paste in an oblong porcelain pâté casserole or oven-ware casserole. Cover top of paste with sliced fat pork; cover casserole with foil and casserole top. Place casserole in pan of water and bake in a 450°F oven for about 50 minutes. Store in refrigerator. Serve as appetizer with crisp crackers or toast rounds. Yield: 3/4 pound.

Fillets of Sole Ostendaise

- 1/2 pound fresh mushrooms or 1 4 1/2-ounce can
- 1 tablespoon minced onion
- 2 tablespoons butter
- 1 tablespoon minced parsley
- 1 teaspoon salt
- 12 oysters
- 1 teaspoon lemon juice
- 1 6-ounce can whole clams
- 12 small pieces of sole
- 12 shrimp, cooked and deveined

Sauce:

- 4 tablespoons flour
- 3 tablespoons melted butter
- Liquid from fillets
- 3 egg yolks
- 1 cup cream
- 1/4 cup sherry

Simmer mushrooms and onions in butter; add parsley and salt. Cook oysters in their juice to which 1 teaspoon lemon juice has been added. Heat clams in their juice. Place fillets in frying pan or skillet; combine clam, oyster, and mushroom juices; add water to make 2 cups and pour over fillets. Simmer for 12 minutes. Remove fillets to serving dish; place clams, oysters, and mushrooms around fillets.

To make the sauce: combine flour and melted butter, cook until brown; add fillet liquid. Cook over low heat, stirring constantly until thick. Combine egg yolks and cream; add to first mixture and heat but do not boil; add sherry.

Pour sauce over fillets; garnish with parsley and shrimp. Yield: 6 servings.

Gateau Wallon (Apple Pie)

- ¼ cup soft butter
- ¼ cup sugar
- ½ teaspoon salt
- 1 cup flour
- 1 egg, well beaten
- 2 cups thick apple sauce, sweetened
- 1 cup confectioners sugar
- Grated rind of 1 lemon
- 3 drops lemon juice
- 1 egg white
- ¼ cup chopped almonds

Cream butter, sugar, and salt; add flour and blend well. Add egg and mix; refrigerate for 2 to 3 hours. Divide dough in half; roll ⅛-inch thick and to fit a 6 x 8 inch baking pan or dish. Line pan with dough; add apple sauce about ¾-inch thick. Cover with other half of dough rolled thin.

Combine confectioners sugar, lemon rind, juice, and enough egg white to make a thick paste. Spread over crust and sprinkle with almonds. Bake in 400°F oven for 30 minutes. Yield: 6 servings.

BOLIVIA

Potatoes a la Huancaina

- 6 medium potatoes, peeled
- Salted water
- 1 4-ounce jar peanut butter
- ¾ cup water
- Salt
- ½ to 1 teaspoon cayenne pepper
- 6 small thin slices cheese (Muenster or Swiss)
- 6 lettuce leaves
- 6 slices of tomato
- 6 slices of hard-boiled egg
- Parsley twigs

Cut potatoes in half lengthwise and cook in boiling salted water until done.

Blend peanut butter and water; add salt and pepper; heat to boiling.

Place a slice of cheese between each two potato halves; place each potato sandwich on a lettuce leaf, pour on sauce. Garnish with tomato, egg, and parsley. Serve hot. Yield: 6 servings.

Spicy Pork Chops

- 6 pork chops
- 1 onion, finely chopped
- 1 clove garlic, minced
- 1 teaspoon salt
- 2 cups water
- ¼ teaspoon cumin seed, ground
- ½-1 teaspoon cayenne pepper
- ½ cup bread crumbs, finely ground

Simmer the pork chops, onion and garlic in salted water until meat is tender. Add cumin seed, pepper and bread crumbs. Simmer and stir for a few minutes until smooth and well blended. Yield: 6 servings.

Meat Empañadas

Dough:

- 4 tablespoons fat
- 1½ cups flour
- 1 tablespoon oil
- 2 eggs
- 2½ tablespoons water

Filling:

- 1 small onion, chopped
- ½ clove garlic, crushed
- ½ cup green pepper, diced
- ½ cup red pepper, diced
- 3 tablespoons fat
- ½ pound chopped beef
- ¼ cup raisins
- ½ cup beef stock
- ½ teaspoon salt
- Few grains pepper
- ½ teaspoon chili powder
- 2 tablespoons flour
- 2 tablespoons water

2 to 3 cups oil for deep-fat frying

Blend the fat and flour in mixing bowl; add the oil and 1 egg beaten. Mix well and gradually add water until dough has a smooth consistency. Cover the dough and refrigerate for an hour. Roll on floured board to approximately 1/16-inch in thickness. Cut into 4-inch circles. Brush each circle with well beaten egg.

For the filling: sauté the onion, garlic, green and red peppers in the hot fat; add the meat and brown lightly, stirring constantly. Stir in the raisins and stock. Simmer until the mixture is done. Add salt, pepper and chili powder. Make a paste of the flour and water; add half to meat mixture, stirring constantly. Add additional paste, if needed to make thick mixture; cool the mixture.

Place 1 heaping tablespoon of meat mixture in the center of each circle; fold the dough to form a half circle. Press the edges together firmly. Fry in deep fat at 375°F until brown. Serve as appetizers. Yield: 1 dozen Empañadas.

BRAZIL

Galinha com Recheio de Castanha
(Chicken with Chestnut Dressing)

1 roasting chicken, 4 to 5 pounds
1 cup white wine
1 clove garlic, minced
Juice of 1 lemon
1½ teaspoons salt
1 tablespoon chopped chives or green onion tops
1 tablespoon minced parsley
Giblets, chopped
1 tablespoon butter
⅛ teaspoon pepper
⅛ teaspoon nutmeg
8-ounces canned purée of chestnuts,
4 slices bacon

Marinate chicken in mixture of wine, garlic, lemon juice, 1 teaspoon salt, chives, and parsley 24 hours in the refrigerator. Drain and wipe chicken dry.

Cook chopped giblets in butter; add pepper, nutmeg, chestnuts and ½ teaspoon salt. Place this mixture inside chicken; place slices of bacon over breast; wrap in foil and place in open roast pan, breast side up. Cook in 375°F oven for 2 hours; open foil covering, brown and complete cooking. Yield: 4-6 servings.

Pudim de Morangos (Strawberry Cream Mold)

½ cup water
1 package strawberry gelatin
2 tablespoons sugar
½ pint heavy cream
2 egg whites, beaten
1 pint fresh strawberries, sliced

Boil water; add gelatin and cool. Add sugar to cream and whip. Fold gelatin into whipped cream; fold in beaten egg whites and sliced strawberries. Pour into doughnut-shaped mold. Let set in refrigerator. Yield: 6 servings.

BULGARIA

Meat Ball Soup

3 chicken bouillon cubes
3 beef bouillon cubes
6 cups boiling water
3 tablespoons rice
1 pound ground lean beef
2 eggs
1 teaspoon salt
¼ teaspoon pepper
1 teaspoon chopped parsley or ½ teaspoon dried
1 small onion, chopped
2 eggs
¼ cup yogurt
1 teaspoon chopped parsley

Add bouillon cubes to boiling water; when dissolved add rice; cover and simmer until rice is tender. Strain rice from bouillon. Combine rice, ground beef, eggs, salt, pepper, parsley, and onion. Make into small balls, about the size of a walnut, and drop into boiling bouillon. Add water, if necessary, to make 4 cups. Simmer gently for 15 minutes.

Beat 2 eggs; combine slowly with small amount of soup until 2 cups have been used. Stir egg and soup mixture into remaining soup; add yogurt. Serve meat balls in soup; sprinkle with chopped parsley. Yield: 6 servings.

Baked Hash with Yogurt Topping

1 onion, diced
2 tablespoons fat
2 pounds ground lean beef
1 teaspoon salt
¼ teaspoon pepper
Few grains cayenne pepper

Brown onion in hot fat; add the meat, seasonings, parsley, and tomato sauce. Simmer for about 15 minutes, stirring occasionally. Add potatoes and hot water to meat mixture; simmer for 10 minutes. Turn mixture into roasting pan, about 10 x 14 inches. Bake for 30 minutes, or until browned in a 375°F oven.

Combine yogurt, eggs, flour, and salt; spread evenly over browned meat. Return to oven to brown for about 10 minutes. Yield: 6-8 servings.

BURMA

Kyet-U-Hin (Egg Curry)

- 3 cups minced onions
- 3 cloves garlic, minced
- ½ teaspoon ginger powder
- 4 tablespoons oil
- 1 teaspoon salt
- ½ teaspoon turmeric
- 1 teaspoon paprika
- 1 cup tomato purée
- 1 cup water
- 1 tablespoon Shrimp Sauce or Fish Soy Sauce
- 6 hard-cooked eggs, cut in halves lengthwise

Cook onions, garlic, and ginger in oil over low heat until onions are done, but not browned. Stir in salt, turmeric, and paprika. Gradually add purée mixed with the water; bring to boiling point and add Shrimp Sauce and egg halves. Cook over low heat until sauce and oil appear to separate and egg whites are tinged with color of sauce. Serve over hot rice. Yield: 6 servings of 1 egg per serving.

Note: Shrimp Sauce (consistency of paste) and Fish Soy Sauce are available at Asiatic import shops. Both are of strong flavor.

Pa-Zun Hin (Prawn Curry)

- 12 medium prawns, shelled and deveined
- 1 tablespoon Shrimp Sauce or Fish Soy Sauce
- ½ teaspoon turmeric
- 1 teaspoon paprika
- 3 cups minced onions
- 3 cloves garlic, minced
- ½ teaspoon ginger
- 4 tablespoons oil
- 1 cup tomato purée
- 1 cup water

Combine prawns, Shrimp Sauce, turmeric and paprika and marinate for 1 hour. Cook minced onions, garlic, and ginger in oil for about 2 minutes. Add prawn mixture to onion mixture; stir occasionally to cook prawns evenly. When prawns are almost done, add tomato purée mixed with water. Cook over low heat until sauce and oil appear to separate. Serve over hot rice. Yield: 6 servings.

BURUNDI

Ibiharage (Fried Beans)

2 cups dry white beans
Boiling water
½ cup cooking oil
3 large onions, sliced
1 clove garlic, minced
2 teaspoons salt
1 or 2 dried hot red peppers

Wash beans and remove any foreign matter. Put beans in large sauce pan and cover with 2 or 3 times as much boiling water as beans; boil 2 minutes; remove from heat and soak 1 hour or more; simmer in the same water until tender. Heat oil to smoking point in a 12-inch sauce pan; add onions and garlic to hot fat and cook until onions are transparent and soft. Drain cooked beans and add to onions; cook for 5 minutes. Add salt and hot peppers; mix well. Yield: 8 to 10 servings.

BYELORUSSIAN SOVIET SOCIALIST REPUBLIC

Machanca (Pork and Sausage with Sour Cream)

1 pound boneless shoulder pork, cut in ½-inch cubes
¾ pound bulk sausage, pork
1 tablespoon fat
1 large onion, diced
2 cups water
4 tablespoons minced parsley
1 tablespoon flour mixed with ¼ cup cold water
¾ cup sour cream

Brown pork and sausage in fat in frying pan. Add onions and cook for 3 minutes, stirring constantly. Add water to meat mixture and stir to loosen meat sticking to bottom of pan and to combine ingredients. Add parsley.

Add flour paste to meat, stirring constantly until well mixed. Cover; simmer for 15 minutes, stirring occasionally. Add more water if necessary to prevent mixture from sticking to pan. When done, add sour cream, heat but do not boil. Serve with pancakes or noodles. Yield: 6 servings.

Chicken Breast Fillets

- 3 chicken breasts with wings attached
- 1 teaspoon salt
- ½ teaspoon pepper

Stuffing:

- ½ pound chicken livers
- ½ cup finely chopped onion
- 1½ tablespoons butter
- Salt and pepper
- 2 to 3 tablespoons sour cream

- 2 eggs
- 4 tablespoons water
- 1½ to 2 cups finely rolled dry bread crumbs
- ½ cup butter
- 2 cups water
- 2 tablespoons flour mixed with 2 tablespoons cold water

To prepare breasts for stuffing, split down center; remove breast bone and cut breasts into halves. Remove tips of wings. Make a 2 to 3 inch slit in each fillet above the rib bones on the under wing side of breast. Sprinkle with salt and pepper.

To make stuffing: cook liver and onion in melted butter over low heat for 10 to 15 minutes. When done, chop or mash liver and onion until fine and blended. Place in small bowl; add salt and pepper to taste and sour cream to give consistency similar to chicken dressing.

Place equal portions of stuffing in slit of each fillet. Stuff in well and secure slit if necessary with toothpick or small skewer. Beat eggs slightly in shallow dish and stir in water. Put bread crumbs in a second shallow dish. Dip fillets first in egg mixture, then into crumbs. Dip each fillet again in both egg mixture and bread crumbs, coating well each time.

Cook fillets in melted butter in large frying pan until brown, about 5 minutes on each side. When brown, add water. Cover; simmer gently for 30 minutes or until meat is tender. Add water, if needed. Remove chicken to serving platter and thicken remaining liquid with paste of flour and water, using only enough to thicken sauce. Blend and simmer 3 minutes. Serve sauce over chicken or in separate sauce dish. Yield: 6 servings.

CAMBODIA

Chicken Soup with Lime

- 2 pounds chicken breasts and thighs
- 2 tablespoons rice
- 1 clove garlic, crushed
- 2 tablespoons chopped chives or green onions
- Water
- ¼ teaspoon monosodium glutamate
- 1 teaspoon salt
- ¼ teaspoon pepper
- 1 teaspoon sugar
- 4 tablespoons lime juice
- 2 tablespoons chopped fresh mint leaves or ½ teaspoon dried mint leaves
- Fish sauce

Have the butcher cut the chicken in bite-size pieces, cutting through bone and meat. Put chicken, rice, garlic, and chives in stew pan; cover with water. Add the monosodium glutamate, salt, and pepper. Cover tightly and boil gently until the chicken is tender. Stir in sugar and lime juice; heat and add mint just before serving. Serve with fish sauce. Yield: 6 servings.

Steak à la Cambodia

- 2 pounds sirloin steak, ¾-inch thick
- 3 tablespoons Soy sauce
- 2 tablespoons fish sauce
- ¼ teaspoon monosodium glutamate
- ¼ teaspoon coarsely ground black pepper
- 1 tablespoon sugar
- 1 teaspoon finely chopped garlic
- 2 tablespoons chopped, roasted peanuts

Marinate the steak for 1 hour in sauce made of all ingredients with the exception of the roasted peanuts. Turn steak frequently so that both sides of steak will be well seasoned.

To broil steak, rub a piece of fat over the broiler rack; place meat on rack about 2 inches from the heat. Broil about 8 minutes on each side for well done steak; 6 minutes for medium, and 5 minutes for rare. Place steak on hot platter. Add remaining marinade and peanuts to meat juices from the broiler; heat and pour over steak. Yield: 4 to 6 servings.

Note: Sherry may be substituted for fish sauce.

Cary au Jus de Coco
(Chicken in Spicy Coconut Sauce)

4 small onions, cut into eighths
1 teaspoon finely chopped garlic
1 tablespoon margarine
2 tablespoons curry powder
1 tablespoon chili powder
2 teaspoons salt
3 cups coconut milk (See Note)
2 2-pound chickens, quartered
4 large potatoes, peeled and cubed
½ cup roasted peanuts

Cook onions and garlic in margarine until onions are soft and yellow. Stir in curry and chili powders, and salt and mix well. Add 2 cups of the coconut milk, chicken, and potatoes. Cover tightly and simmer 20 to 30 minutes or until chicken is tender. Add remaining cup of coconut milk and peanuts. Simmer for 10 minutes and serve. Yield: 6 servings.

Note: To make Coconut Milk: combine 4 ounces packaged coconut with 1 quart milk; let stand in refrigerator over night. Drain off milk; squeeze or mash coconut to get full flavor. Discard coconut.

CAMEROON

Fish Stew with Rice

2 slices onion
⅓ cup oil
3 tablespoons tomato paste
2½ pounds of fish, boned and in large pieces
1 quart water
2 teaspoons salt
2 carrots, sliced
½ pound cabbage, shredded
2 small sweet potatoes, cut in 1-inch cubes
½ package frozen okra
3 cups cooked rice

Cook onion in hot oil in a 4-quart saucepan until yellow but not brown; add tomato paste and fish. Cover; cook over low heat ½ hour. Add water, salt, and vegetables to fish mixture; cook gently for 1 hour.

Place a serving of rice in the center of a soup bowl or plate; ladle stew over rice, serving some fish, vegetables, and broth. Yield: 6 servings.

CANADA

Sucre à la Crème (Sugar Cream Confection)

- 2 pounds brown sugar or maple sugar
- ½ cup heavy cream
- ¼ pound butter
- 1 cup walnuts, coarsely chopped

Combine sugar and cream in a 2-quart sauce pan; bring to a boil quickly, stirring constantly. Lower heat to simmer; add butter and continue stirring until butter melts. Remove from fire and add chopped walnuts. Beat until thick and creamy. Pour into a buttered pan. Let cool and cut into 1-inch squares. Yield: 2 pounds.

Soupe à la Morue (Codfish Soup)

- 1 pound codfish, fresh or frozen
- 1 teaspoon salt
- 1½ cups water
- 1 cup diced raw potatoes
- ½ teaspoon salt
- ½ cup water
- 2 tablespoons fat
- 2 tablespoons flour
- ½ teaspoon salt
- Pepper
- 3 cups milk
- ¼ cup finely chopped onion
- 2 tablespoons finely chopped chives

Boil codfish in salted water for 15 to 20 minutes, or according to directions on package. Drain. Boil potatoes in salted water for 10 to 15 minutes. Drain. Prepare a thin white sauce: melt fat, add flour, salt, and pepper. Blend and add milk, stirring constantly. Transfer sauce to a double boiler. Add crumbled codfish, potatoes, onion, and chives. Cook in double boiler for 20 to 30 minutes. Serve hot. Yield: 6 servings.

Tourtière de la Gaspesie

(Three Meats Pie)

- 1 3½-pound stewing chicken, cut in pieces
- 4 cups water
- ½ pound ground fresh pork
- ½ pound ground beef
- ¼ cup chopped onion
- 2 cloves garlic, minced
- 1½ cups water
- 2 teaspoons salt
- ½ teaspoon pepper
- Dough for 2 pie crusts

Sauce:

- ¼ cup flour
- ½ cup water
- 2½ cups broth

Simmer chicken pieces in water for 2 to 3 hours or until tender. Remove chicken; drain and save broth.

Simmer pork, beef, onion, and half the garlic in water for 15 to 20 minutes. Drain and save broth.

Remove chicken from bone; grind and combine with pork and beef mixture, salt, pepper, and remaining garlic, and ¼ cup of the chicken broth. Place in 9-inch pie shell; spread evenly; cover with top crust; make slits. Bake for 40 to 45 minutes or until crust is golden brown in a 400°F oven. Serve with sauce.

To make sauce: combine flour and water; add to hot broth and simmer 5 minutes. Yield: 8 servings.

Butter Tarts

Pastry:

- 2 cups flour
- 1 teaspoon salt
- ¾ cup hydrogenated shortening
- 5 tablespoons ice water

Tart Filling:

- 2 eggs, beaten slightly
- 2 cups brown sugar
- 2 tablespoons vinegar
- 1 tablespoon vanilla
- ½ cup melted butter
- 1⅓ cups currants, raisins, dates, figs, or nuts

- ½ cup heavy cream, whipped with sugar

To make pastry: sift flour and salt; blend fat into flour until mixture particles are the size of small peas. Add water; mix with a fork. Knead dough slightly to form smooth ball. Roll dough out and cut to fit tart pans, 3 to 4 inches in size.

To make tart filling: combine eggs, sugar, vinegar, and vanilla; stir in melted fat and fruits or nuts (various combinations may be used).

Fill tart shells one-half to two-thirds full. Bake for 10 minutes in a 450°F oven; reduce heat to 325°F and cook for 20 to 25 minutes. Top each tart with sweetened whipped cream and serve as dessert. Yield: 6-8 tarts.

CENTRAL AFRICAN REPUBLIC

Spinach à l'Afrique

- 2 onions, chopped
- 2 tablespoons oil
- 2 tomatoes, thinly sliced
- 1 green pepper, chopped
- 2 packages of chopped frozen spinach, thawed
- 1 teaspoon salt
- 1/8 teaspoon pepper
- 1/2 cup peanut butter

Sauté onions in oil until tender; add tomatoes and green pepper and cook for 1 minute. Add spinach, salt, and pepper; cover and simmer for 5 minutes. Add peanut butter to spinach mixture; combine well and cook for 10 minutes over low heat. Stir occasionally to prevent sticking. Serve hot. Yield: 6 servings.

CEYLON

Deviled Fish

- 1 large onion, chopped
- 1 tablespoon oil
- 1 tablespoon dry mustard
- 2 teaspoons chili powder
- 1 bay leaf
- 1 teaspoon salt
- 1 tablespoon Worcestershire Sauce
- 2 teaspoons sugar
- 1 cup light cream or coconut milk (page 27)
- 2 tablespoons vinegar
- 1 pound fish fillets, canned salmon, or tuna fish

Cook onion in oil until yellow. Add seasonings, except vinegar, and blend; add cream or milk and stir until sauce is smooth. Add vinegar slowly.

If fresh fish is used, boil for 5 minutes in salted water and drain; if frozen fillets are used, follow directions on package; if canned fish is used, drain off oil. Add fish in large pieces to sauce and heat. Yield: 4 to 6 servings.

Soup Mulligatawny (Chicken Soup)

- 2½ pound stewing chicken, cut into serving pieces
- 2 teaspoons salt
- 6 cups cold water
- ½ teaspoon coriander seeds
- 1 teaspoon cumin seeds
- ½ teaspoon powdered ginger
- 1 bay leaf
- 1 stick cinnamon
- 10 peppercorns
- 1 clove garlic, crushed
- 1 cup canned tomatoes
- 1 medium onion, chopped
- 2 teaspoons fat
- 2 tablespoons lemon juice
- 1 cup light cream or coconut milk (page 27)

Stew chicken in salted water in large covered sauce pan. After 30 minutes, add seasonings, tomatoes, and half of the onion. Continue cooking over low heat until chicken is tender. Add water, if necessary. Remove chicken and strain stock. Brown remaining onion in fat. Add chicken, browned onion, lemon juice, and cream to stock. Reheat, but do not boil mixture. Yield: 4 to 6 servings.

CHAD

Squash with Peanuts

2½ to 3 pounds summer squash or zucchini
Salt
Water
1 cup shelled, roasted peanuts
2 tablespoons fat
1 teaspoon sugar, optional

Wash squash; cut off stems; do not pare. Cook in a small amount of boiling salted water, or steam until tender. Drain well and mash.

Chop peanuts coarsely, or use a meat grinder or blender. Combine squash, peanuts, fat, and sugar if desired. Simmer and serve hot. Yield: 6 servings.

Meat and Okra Sauce

2 pounds cubed beef or lamb
2 tablespoons fat
1 medium onion, chopped
1 teaspoon salt
1 6-ounce can tomato paste
8 fresh okra pods or ½ of 10-ounce package frozen okra

Brown meat in fat. Add onion and cook until yellow. Add salt, and tomato paste diluted with equal amount of water. Cover; simmer about 1½ hours or until meat is tender. Add water as needed. Add okra 30 minutes before end of cooking period. Serve as a sauce with boiled rice. Yield: 6 servings.

CHILE

Gallina en Escabeche (Chicken Mold)

¼ cup olive oil
3 pounds chicken breasts, boned, skinned, and quartered
2 medium onions, sliced and rings separated
3 large carrots, sliced
3 tablespoons pimiento, chopped
12 peppercorns
1 teaspoon salt
1 cup dry white wine

Dressing:

½ cup oil from cooked chicken
½ cup olive oil
¼ cup vinegar
1 teaspoon tomato juice
¼ teaspoon salt
Few grains cayenne pepper

Pour the oil in a heavy pot or kettle with a tightly fitting lid. Arrange a layer of breast quarters symmetrically in the oil, using ⅓ of the chicken. Place a layer of ⅓ of the onion rings, carrot slices, pimiento, peppercorns, and salt over the chicken. Repeat, making second and third set of layers. Place the chicken bones over the top layer; add the wine. Cover the pot tightly and simmer gently for 3 hours. When done, remove the bones; cool the chicken in the uncovered pot. When cool, replace cover and refrigerate over night. Remove excess oil and use for the salad dressing. Return the chicken to the refrigerator until serving time.

To make dressing: combine all ingredients and keep in refrigerator.

Unmold chicken on platter or chop dish. Serve with the dressing and garnish with fresh greens and black olives. Yield: 6 servings.

Sopaipillas Chilenitas (Squash Fritters)

1 pound squash
1 stick cinnamon
½ cup water
5 cups sifted flour
1 tablespoon salt
1 tablespoon oil
Boiling water

Fat for frying

Syrup:

1½ cups brown sugar
3 tablespoons white sugar
1 stick cinnamon
1 orange rind, cut in thin strips
1 whole clove
¾ cup water

Cook the squash and cinnamon in water until squash is tender. Remove cinnamon and drain. Mash squash and add sifted flour, salt, and oil. Place on kneading board; add enough boiling water to the mixture to form a dough that will not stick to the board. Knead well, and keep mixture warm. Cut fritter-size pieces from dough and drop into deep fat, 325°F. Cook fritters 2 to 3 minutes or until golden brown. Drain on paper towels.

To make syrup: place syrup ingredients in sauce pan. Stir to dissolve sugars; simmer for about 5 minutes. Keep syrup hot.

Drop fritters in a bowl of the hot syrup and serve. Yield: 36 fritters.

CHINA

3-Cup Chicken

- 3 cups raw chicken, cut from bones
- ⅓ cup oil
- 1 cup sherry
- ½ cup soy sauce
- 4 cloves garlic, minced
- 1 teaspoon powdered ginger
- 3 onions, finely minced
- 1 teaspoon sugar

Place chicken in saucepan; add all of the other ingredients. Liquid should cover chicken. Cover and bring to boiling point; reduce heat and simmer for 40 to 60 minutes or until chicken is tender. Serve with steamed rice. Yield: 6 servings.

Beef and Onions

- 1½ pounds flank, boneless round, or sirloin steak

Marinade:

- ¼ cup cornstarch
- 1 teaspoon sugar
- 3 tablespoons soy sauce or Chinese Oyster Sauce
- 2 teaspoons sherry

- 5 tablespoons oil
- 2 large onions, sliced
- ½ cup chicken broth or bouillon

Slice beef across the grain into thin strips, about ½-inch wide and 3-inches long. To make marinade: combine all ingredients and blend well. Place beef strips in marinade; turn gently, until all pieces are coated. Let marinate for about 5 minutes.

Heat oil in large frying pan and sauté beef for about 2 minutes, stirring constantly. Remove meat to a plate. Cook onion in remaining oil (add more oil, if necessary) until onions are limp or about 2 minutes. Add beef and broth to onions and simmer uncovered for about 3 minutes. Yield: 6 servings.

Chicken with Chestnuts

- 1 3-pound fryer
- 1 teaspoon salt
- Water
- 6 to 8 dried Chinese mushrooms
- 2 ½-inch slices fresh ginger
- 4 tablespoons oil
- ⅓ cup soy sauce
- 1 tablespoon sugar
- 1 tablespoon sherry
- 2 5-ounce cans water chestnuts
- 2 cups chicken broth

Simmer chicken in salted water to cover until tender but firm. Remove chicken from broth; cool; remove from bone and cut into 2-inch pieces. Soak mushrooms in cold water for ½ hour. Fry ginger in hot oil in heavy 12-inch frying pan; add chicken and thinly sliced mushrooms; sauté for 5 minutes. Add soy sauce, sugar, sherry, chestnuts, and broth. Simmer about 15 minutes uncovered; remove ginger slices. Yield: 6 to 8 servings.

Chinese Soup

- 1 chicken, halved
- 1 teaspoon salt
- 6 cups water
- 1 large onion, finely chopped
- ¾ cup finely cubed pork, cooked
- 2 pounds shrimp, cooked and deveined
- 2 cups fresh mushrooms, cleaned and sautéed in 2 tablespoons butter
- ¼ pound transparent Chinese noodles
- 1 teaspoon soy sauce
- ½ pound scallions, finely cut
- 2 cloves garlic, minced
- 2 tablespoons oil
- ½ teaspoon powdered coriander

Simmer chicken in salted water with onion until chicken is tender. Remove chicken from broth; skin and bone chicken; cool and cut meat into long thin slivers. Return chicken to broth; add pork, shrimp, and mushrooms; boil for 5 minutes; add noodles and soy sauce and simmer for 5 minutes.

Sauté scallions and garlic in oil with coriander for 5 minutes; add to soup and serve hot. Yield: 8 servings.

Note: Transparent Chinese noodles are known as Sai Fun in Chinese food shops.

COLOMBIA

Aguacate Picante (Spiced Avocado)

- 2 medium onions
- 1 clove garlic
- 2 large green peppers, seeds and stems removed
- 2 small hot red peppers
- ¼ cup olive oil
- ¼ cup tomato sauce
- ½ cup vinegar
- 1 teaspoon salt
- 3 or 4 large avocados, minced
- ½ pound fried bacon, chopped

Grind onions, garlic, and peppers; cook in hot oil until onions are golden yellow; add the tomato sauce, vinegar, and salt. Simmer mixture for 20 to 30 minutes; cool slightly and gently stir in the avocados and bacon. Yield: 8 servings.

Sopa de Habas (Lima Bean Soup)

- ½ pound meaty beef bones or short ribs
- 1 medium onion, chopped
- 1 large carrot, chopped
- 2 tablespoons chopped parsley
- 1½ cups canned tomatoes
- Water
- 1 12-ounce package frozen green baby lima beans
- ⅓ cup cornstarch
- ⅓ cup milk
- 2 teaspoons salt
- ⅛ teaspoon pepper

Place beef bones, onion, carrot, parsley, and tomatoes in deep soup kettle with water to cover. Cover kettle; bring contents to a broil; reduce heat and simmer until the meat is tender, about 2 hours. Remove meat from bones and return to soup; add the lima beans; simmer for about 20 minutes or until beans are barely tender.

Combine cornstarch and milk; add a small amount of hot liquid from soup to cornstarch and blend well. Add cornstarch paste, salt and pepper to soup. Simmer 10 to 15 minutes to blend flavors. Yield: 6 to 8 servings.

Papas Chorriadas

(Potatoes with Cheese Sauce)

- 6 medium potatoes, pared
- Salt
- Water

Sauce:

- 2 tablespoons fat
- 1 tablespoon flour
- 1 teaspoon salt
- 1 large onion, sliced
- 1 large tomato, sliced
- 1½ cups milk
- ¼ pound Gruyère cheese, grated
- 1 tablespoon heavy cream

Boil potatoes in salted water (2 teaspoons of salt for 1 quart of water) until tender. Drain off water and keep potatoes warm.

To make sauce: melt fat in 8-inch frying pan. Add flour and salt and blend; add onion and tomato. Stir and cook for 3 minutes. Add milk, stirring constantly. Cook over low heat until sauce boils. Add cheese and cream. Stir until cheese melts.

Pour sauce over hot potatoes. Yield: 6 servings.

CONGO (Brazzaville)

Mbisi ye Kalou na Loso (Fish and Collards)

- 1 cup chopped onion
- 1 sweet green pepper, sliced
- 3 tablespoons oil
- ¼ teaspoon black pepper
- ½ teaspoon paprika
- 1 12-ounce package frozen collards or other greens
- 1 cup water
- 6 to 8 tablespoons butter, as desired
- 1½ pounds frozen fish, thawed

Cook onion and green pepper in oil in large frying pan for 5 minutes. Add black pepper, paprika, collards, and water. Cover and simmer for 5 to 10 minutes. Add butter and fish, cut in finger-strips. Cover and simmer for 20 minutes or until fish is tender and flaky. Serve as main course with yams. Yield: 6 servings.

CONGO (Democratic Republic of)

Chicken à la Moambé
(Fried Chicken with Peanut Butter Sauce)

- 1 3-pound fryer, cut for frying
- ½ cup oil
- 1 6-ounce can tomato paste
- 2 6-ounce cans water
- 1½ teaspoons salt
- ½ teaspoon pepper
- ¼ cup peanut butter

Brown chicken pieces in hot fat in a 12-inch frying pan. Drain and discard oil from pan when chicken is browned. Combine tomato paste and water; pour over chicken; loosen chicken from pan and simmer for 10 minutes. Add salt, pepper, and peanut butter; simmer for additional 20 minutes. Yield: 6 servings.

COSTA RICA

Pie de Pollo y Eloté
(Chicken and Corn)

- 5 eggs, beaten
- 2 1-pound cans cream style sweet corn
- 8 ounces Muenster, grated
- 1 chicken, boiled
- 1 cup carrots, cooked and diced
- 1 1-pound can string beans, drained
- 1 1-pound can peas, drained
- 1½ teaspoons salt
- 4 ounces green pitted olives, sliced
- 1 cup chicken stock
- 4 tablespoons raisins
- 2 tablespoons butter
- 1 green pepper, cut in strips
- 1 red pepper, cut in strips

Combine eggs, corn and cheese in a medium bowl.

Remove bones from chicken and cut into small pieces. In another bowl, combine chicken with vegetables, salt, olives, broth and raisins.

Place a layer of corn mixture in a 3-quart oiled casserole; add a layer of the chicken mixture; continue alternating layers, ending with layer of corn. Dot top with butter; garnish with pepper strips in flower-like design. Bake for 40 minutes in a 350°F oven. Yield: 8-10 servings.

Mousse de Aguacate (Avocado Mousse)

- 1 large well-ripened avocado, peeled, seeded, cut in small pieces
- 1 small onion, grated
- ½ teaspoon salt
- ¼ teaspoon Worcestershire Sauce
- 1 tablespoon gelatin
- ¾ cup cold water
- ¼ cup boiling water
- ¼ cup whipped cream
- ¼ cup mayonnaise

Blend the avocado, onion, salt and Worcestershire Sauce until very smooth.

Soften gelatin in ⅓ of the cold water. Add boiling water and stir until dissolved; stir in remaining cold water and cool. When gelatin mixture is consistency of an egg-white, gradually fold in whipped cream, mayonnaise and the avocado mixture. Pour into mold, rinsed with cold water; refrigerate until set. Serve on slices of tomatoes placed on lettuce leaves. Yield: 6 servings.

CUBA

Ropa Vieja (Raggedy Beef Stew)

2 pounds boneless beef, flank or chuck
3 slices bacon or ½ cup diced ham
1 carrot, peeled and sliced
1 turnip, peeled and sliced
1 leek, chopped (onion may be used)
2 quarts water
1 medium-sized onion, diced
1 clove garlic, minced
3 tablespoons margarine
1 green pepper, diced
2 1-pound cans tomatoes
1 bay leaf
2 cloves
1 tablespoon salt
¼ teaspoon pepper
1 teaspoon paprika
1 cup bread crumbs
3 sweet pimientos, diced
Croutons
Parsley

Cut beef into 1-inch cubes; place in 3-quart saucepan. Add bacon or ham, carrot, turnip, and leek or onion. Add water; cover and boil slowly for 3 to 4 hours or until meat shreds easily. Remove meat from saucepan; pound it with meat mallet or edge of heavy saucer until meat is a mass of shreds (Raggedy). Separate fibers with fork, if necessary to shred.

Cook onion and garlic in margarine in large frying pan until yellow. Add green pepper, tomatoes, bay leaf, cloves, salt, pepper, and paprika. Simmer for 10 minutes or until green pepper is soft. Add this mixture to the broth in which meat was cooked. Simmer slowly for 5 minutes to blend flavors. Strain mixture and thicken strained liquid with bread crumbs. Add half of pimientos and shredded meat to thickened stock and simmer slowly for 15-30 minutes. Serve hot, garnish with remaining pimientos, croutons or small triangles of fried bread, and parsley. Yield: 6 servings.

Note: Vegetables may be left in the stew; if not, they may be served as side dish with stew or for another meal.

Coco Quemado (Toasted Coconut Dessert)

2 cups sugar
1 cup water
4 egg yolks, lightly beaten
⅓ cup sherry
½ teaspoon ground cinnamon
1 7-ounce package coconut

Combine sugar and water in a 2-quart saucepan and cook to light or thin syrup consistency or 225°F. Add hot syrup to egg yolks gradually until 1 cup syrup has been added, stirring constantly. Combine with remaining syrup; add sherry, cinnamon and coconut. Cook until mixture begins to boil, stirring constantly. Spread in 9-inch square cake pan and bake ½ hour at 350°F. Serve alone or with vanilla ice cream. Yield: 6 servings.

CYPRUS

Tavá (Lamb and Vegetables)

- 3 pounds lamb shoulder or leg, cut in 1-inch cubes
- 1 pound rice, uncooked
- 2 pounds potatoes, sliced
- 1 pound onions, sliced
- 2 tablespoons salt
- 3/4 teaspoon pepper
- 3 teaspoons cumin powder
- 1 pound zucchini squash, sliced
- 8 artichoke hearts, cut in halves (optional)
- 2 1-pound cans tomatoes

Use a 6-quart oven-proof casserole or Dutch oven. Place approximately one-third of each ingredient in the order listed in the casserole. Repeat for second and third layers. Fill casserole with water. Cover; bake at 350°F for 1½ to 2 hours, or until meat is tender. Add water, if necessary, during cooking. Water should be well absorbed when done. Let casserole stand for 20-30 minutes before it is served. Yield: 6-8 servings.

Afēlia (Pork and Potatoes)

- 3 pounds pork, cut in cubes
- 1½ cups dry red wine
- ¼ cup fat
- 2 pounds potatoes, cut in long strips
- 1 tablespoon salt
- 1 teaspoon pepper
- 1 tablespoon coriander
- 1 cup water

Place pork and wine in bowl. Cover; place in refrigerator for 3 to 4 days, turning meat several times. If time is limited, overnight will give good flavor.

Brown pork in hot fat in Dutch oven or cast aluminum saucepan; remove meat. Brown potato strips in remaining fat and remove. Return meat and place potatoes on top of meat. Add salt, pepper, coriander, and 1 cup water. Cover; simmer for 1 hour over very low fire. Check to prevent burning and add only a small amount of water, if necessary, during cooking period. When meat is tender, remove from heat and add remainder of wine used for marinating pork. Cover; let stand for 10 minutes. Yield: 6-8 servings.

CZECHOSLOVAKIA

Svíčková Pečeně
(Pickled Beef with Sour Cream)

3 pounds rolled rump or rib roast
3 slices bacon
1 teaspoon salt
¼ cup margarine or butter
½ cup diced celery
½ cup diced carrot
2 tablespoons chopped parsley
½ cup diced onion
1 bay leaf
⅛ teaspoon thyme
¼ teaspoon pepper
¼ cup water
¼ cup vinegar
1 tablespoon sugar

Sour Cream Sauce:

¼ cup flour
Juices from meat
1 pint sour cream

Release cord from roast and distribute bacon slices evenly around roast. Roll and re-tie roast; rub with salt and set aside. Melt fat in Dutch oven or heavy ovenware with cover; add celery, carrot, parsley, and onion; cook over low heat for 10 minutes. Stir in bay leaf, thyme, and pepper. Place meat on top of vegetable mixture; cover and simmer for 1 hour. Add water, vinegar and sugar. Cover; place in 350°F oven and bake for 1½ hours or until meat is tender. Add water, when needed. Cut meat in thin slices.

To make Sour Cream Sauce: blend flour with juices in pan in which meat was cooked; simmer for 5 minutes; add sour cream and heat just below boiling. Strain and serve hot with the beef. Yield: 6 servings.

Ovocné Knedlíky (Fruit Dumplings)

1½ tablespoons butter or margarine
4 ounces cottage cheese
1 egg yolk
½ teaspoon salt
¼ cup milk
1¾ cups flour
Fruit, 12 fresh plums or prunes, small apricots, peach halves
Boiling salted water
3 tablespoons melted butter
6 tablespoons sugar

Cream butter, cottage cheese, egg yolk and salt; add milk. Stir in flour, stirring well until dough leaves side of bowl and is not sticky to the touch. Cover and set aside for 30 minutes.

Roll dough on lightly floured board into a rectangle, approximately 9 x 12 inches and ¼-inch thick. Cut into 12 3-inch squares. Place a piece of fruit (pitted) in the center of each square. Wrap dough around fruit into a round ball. Drop dumplings into a 6-quart saucepan of boiling salted water. Cover; cook dumplings for 8 minutes; remove and drain. Sprinkle with melted butter and sugar. Serve as dessert. Yield: 6 servings.

DAHOMEY

Wonders Dessert

- $1\frac{3}{4}$ cups flour
- 1 teaspoon salt
- 6 tablespoons butter
- $\frac{1}{4}$ cup water
- 1 tablespoon oil
- Fat for frying
- $\frac{1}{2}$ cup sugar
- $\frac{1}{2}$ teaspoon cinnamon or mace

Combine flour and salt in mixing bowl, cut in the butter until mixture resembles coarse meal. Stir in ½ of the water; add the remainder and the oil; mix only until dough holds together when pressed. Place dough on floured board and knead gently 8 to 10 times. Roll dough into ¼-inch thickness; cut into strips of various widths and about 2-inches long or into triangles or circles. Fry in 1-inch fat in heavy frying pan at 375°F, turning once, until delicately browned on both sides and cooked throughout, 8 to 10 minutes. Drain on absorbent paper. Dust with mixture of sugar and spice. Serve warm or cold as dessert or snacks. Yield: 6 servings.

Note: For large-scale recipe, roll ¼ of dough at a time, keeping remainder covered.

Beef and Shrimp in Spinach Sauce

- 1 pound stew meat, cut into 1-inch cubes
- $\frac{1}{2}$ teaspoon salt
- $\frac{1}{4}$ teaspoon pepper
- 1 clove garlic, cut in half
- 1 cup diced onions
- Water
- 2 10-ounce packages frozen chopped spinach
- 3 tablespoons oil
- 4 tomatoes, seeds removed, and diced
- $\frac{1}{2}$ pound shrimp, shelled and deveined
- $\frac{1}{2}$ teaspoon powdered thyme

Place meat, salt, pepper, garlic, and ½ of the diced onions in a 3-quart saucepan. Cover with water; cover saucepan and simmer for 2 hours or until meat is tender.

Cook frozen spinach according to package directions; drain well. Heat oil in a 12-inch skillet; cook remaining half of onions and tomatoes until onion is transparent. Add shrimp and thyme to the onion and tomato mixture and simmer for 10 minutes. Add the cooked beef with liquid and drained spinach to the shrimp mixture. Simmer for 5 minutes or until sauce is thick, stirring occasionally.

Serve with hot rice. Yield: 6 servings.

DENMARK

Rødkaal (Red Cabbage)

- 2 pounds red cabbage
- 2 tablespoons butter or margarine
- 1 tablespoon sugar
- 3 tablespoons red currant jelly
- 2 tablespoons vinegar

Remove wilted outer leaves. Cut in quarters; cut out the core. Rinse with cold water; drain and shred very fine. Melt fat in large saucepan; add sugar, jelly, and vinegar. Blend and add shredded cabbage. Cover tightly; simmer until cabbage is very tender, stirring occasionally. Serve with pork or pot roast. Yield: 6 servings.

Ris a l'Amande (Rice Dessert with Cherry Sauce)

- 2 cups milk
- 1/4 cup white rice
- 1/4 teaspoon salt
- 1 teaspoon gelatine
- 2 tablespoons cold milk
- 1 tablespoon butter
- 1/4 cup sugar
- 1/3 cup blanched almonds, chopped
- 1 teaspoon vanilla
- 1 tablespoon sherry
- 1/2 cup heavy sweet cream

Kirsebaersauce (Cherry Sauce):

- 1 1-pound can dark, sweet cherries, pitted
- 1 tablespoon cornstarch
- 1 tablespoon lemon juice or 1/4 teaspoon almond extract

Scald milk in 2-quart saucepan. Add rice and salt; cover tightly and simmer for one hour, stirring occasionally. Remove from heat. Dissolve gelatine in cold milk; add gelatine mixture, butter and sugar to hot rice and milk mixture. When cooled, add almonds, vanilla, and sherry. Beat cream until stiff; fold into rice mixture. Pour into 6 individual serving dishes or 1 large mold. Chill for several hours; serve very cold, plain or with cherry sauce.

To make Cherry Sauce: strain juice from cherries into a saucepan; add other fruit juice or water if needed to make 1 cup. Mix cornstarch with 2 tablespoons of the fruit juice; add to remainder of juice. Stir the mixture over low heat for 5 minutes. Remove from heat and add lemon juice or almond extract. When cooled, add cherries and chill in refrigerator. Store in tightly covered glass jar, if to be kept several days. Serve also with vanilla blanc mange, custard, or bread pudding. Yield: 6 servings.

DOMINICAN REPUBLIC

Pastelitos (Little Meat Pies)

Pastry:

2 egg yolks
4 tablespoons butter, softened
½ cup water
2 cups sifted flour
2 teaspoons salt
½ teaspoon soda

Filling:

1 pound lean pork or boned chicken
2 ounces smoked ham
1 teaspoon salt
¼ teaspoon pepper
¼ teaspoon oregano
1 clove garlic, crushed
1 small onion, chopped
2 teaspoons vinegar
1 bay leaf
2 tablespoons parsley
2 tablespoons oil
2 tablespoons tomato paste
½ cup water
1 teaspoon capers
2 tablespoons raisins
8 chopped ripe olives
2 hard-cooked eggs

3 cups oil for frying

To make the pastry: blend yolks and butter; add water and sifted flour, salt, and soda, alternately to egg and butter mixture. Wrap in waxed paper and place in refrigerator for an hour.

To make filling: grind meats together; add salt, pepper, oregano, garlic, onion, vinegar, bay leaf, and parsley to ground meats. Add seasoned meat to hot oil in skillet and cook until brown; stir frequently. Add tomato paste and water to meat mixture; stir well; cover and cook slowly for 25 minutes. Add capers and raisins and cook slowly for 5 minutes; add olives and eggs; mix well.

To make pastelitos, roll ¼ of the pastry dough on a lightly floured board to about ⅛-inch thickness. Cut pastry into 2-inch squares. Place a teaspoon of meat mixture in center of half of pastry squares; moisten edges with water; cover with another pastry square; press edges together and seal. Continue until filling and pastry are used. Deep-fat fry in hot oil until pastelitos are brown. Serve as appetizers. Yield: 60-70 pastelitos.

Sopa de Frijoles (Hearty Bean Soup)

- 1 pound dried beans, pinto or kidney
- 2 quarts boiling water
- 1 pound salt pork, cut into 6 slices
- 4 slices bacon, cut into 1-inch pieces
- ¼ pound bulk or link sausage
- 3 cloves garlic, mashed
- 1 large onion, chopped
- 1 teaspoon chili powder
- 2 drops Tabasco
- 2 tablespoons salt
- 2 tablespoons vinegar
- 2 tablespoons tomato paste
- 2 green bananas, sliced

Wash the beans and place in a 4-quart kettle. Add boiling water to beans, cover, and let boil 2 minutes. Remove from heat and let beans soak for 1 hour in same water.

Cook salt pork, bacon, and sausage over low heat for 10 minutes. Remove meat from fat and add to bean pot. Cook garlic and chopped onions in remaining fat until yellow. Drain and add to beans. Cover and simmer over low heat for 2 hours. Stir occasionally. Add seasonings and sliced bananas to bean mixture and simmer for another hour or until beans and bananas are tender and soup is thick. Skim off excess fat and serve hot. Yield: 6-8 servings.

ECUADOR

Seviche (Pickled Fish)

- 1½ pounds thin fillets of bass or any delicate fish
- ¾ cup lemon juice
- ⅓ cup orange juice
- 2 tablespoons tomato catsup
- 1 medium onion, chopped
- 1 chili pepper, minced
- 1 sweet red pepper, chopped
- 1 sweet green pepper, chopped
- ¼ cup corn kernels
- ½ teaspoon salt

Lay thin fillets on a platter side-by-side; cover with ⅔ of the lemon juice. Cover and place in refrigerator over night.

Drain fillets and place on serving platter. Combine all other ingredients into a sauce; spread over fillets and serve as an appetizer. Yield: 6-8 servings.

EL SALVADOR

Gallina en Chicha
(Chicken in Wine Sauce)

1 5-pound chicken
2 large onions, sliced
1 tablespoon salt
Water
2 tablespoons sesame seeds
2 sweet red peppers (dried)
2 peppercorns
4 small laurel leaves
1 small Italian bread loaf soaked in sweet Red Table wine
1 cup apple vinegar
1 teaspoon black pepper
1 cup sweet Red Table wine
1 tablespoon Worcestershire sauce
24 dried prunes, pitted
1 cup olives, pitted
½ cup capers
2 small cans tomato paste
1 can pimientos, cut into strips
1 cup sugar

Cut the chicken into serving pieces and simmer slowly with onions in salted water, using only enough water to cover bottom of skillet. Add water as needed.

Grind into a paste the sesame seeds, red peppers, peppercorns, laurel leaves, and the bread soaked in wine.

When the chicken is soft, add the vinegar, black pepper, wine, Worcestershire sauce, prunes, olives, capers, tomato paste, pimientos, sugar and the sesame seed paste. Cover and cook slowly on top of stove for 1 hour. Yield: 6 servings.

Sopa de Frijoles (Bean Soup)

1 pound red beans, cooked
8 cups water
1 teaspoon salt
¾ cup onion, chopped very fine
2 tablespoons oil
1 dash powdered clove
1 dash cinnamon
1 dash pepper
1 dash thyme
¼ teaspoon oregano
6 slices white bread, quartered

Boil beans in salted water for 2 minutes. Remove from heat and let soak for 2 hours. Cook beans in same water until soft. Remove and mash 3 tablespoons of cooked beans and return to broth.

Sauté the onion in 1 tablespoon of oil and add to broth. Add seasonings and boil for 10 minutes.

Sauté bread in remaining oil until brown and place in individual soup plates, add the soup and serve. Yield: 8 servings.

ETHIOPIA

Retfo (Ground Beef with Peppers)

- 1 large onion, diced
- 1 medium green pepper, diced
- 3 tablespoons margarine
- 1½ pounds ground beef
- 1 or 2 dried hot peppers or ¼ teaspoon crushed red pepper
- 1½ teaspoons salt
- ¼ teaspoon pepper

Cook onion and green pepper in margarine in a 10-inch skillet until onion is yellow and pepper is tender. Add ground beef to cooked vegetables and cook over medium heat for about 3 minutes. Crush red peppers; mix with salt and pepper and add to meat mixture. Continue cooking until meat is brown. Serve with rice. Yield: 6 servings.

FINLAND

Pappilan Hätävara (Lingonberry Shortcake)

- ¼ cup powdered sugar
- 2 cups heavy cream, whipped
- 1 cup lingonberry preserves
- 1 5-ounce package rusks
- 12 to 18 vanilla wafers
- 1 cup milk

Fold powdered sugar into whipped cream. Place alternate layers of cream, fruit preserves, a rusk and a cooky dipped in milk in individual dessert dishes. Continue layers with cream as top layer. Refrigerate and serve very cold. Yield: 6-8 servings.

Note: Other fruit preserves or fresh, frozen, or canned fruit may be used.

Kesäkeitto (Summer Vegetable Soup)

4 small carrots, diced
¾ cup green peas
½ small cauliflower, diced or broken in small flowerlets
3 small, new potatoes, diced
½ cup string beans, sliced
4 radishes, cut in half
Boiling water
2 teaspoons salt
1½ tablespoons sugar
2 cups chopped spinach
1½ tablespoons butter
1½ tablespoons flour
1 egg yolk
1 pint milk
¼ cup cream
1 cup shrimp, cooked and deveined

Combine all prepared vegetables, except spinach, in a large kettle; cover with boiling water; add salt and sugar and simmer about 45 minutes. Add spinach and simmer for 10 minutes. Combine melted butter and flour in second kettle; combine egg, milk, and cream and stir into butter and flour. Add cooked vegetables and liquid (not more than 1 pint). Add shrimp and heat. Serve hot immediately. Yield: 6 servings.

Mantelikokkare
(Almond Custard with Huckleberry Sauce)

½ cup sugar
¼ teaspoon salt
2½ tablespoons cornstarch or 4½ tablespoons flour
4 eggs, beaten slightly
1 quart milk, scalded
1 teaspoon almond extract

Mustikkakeitto (Huckleberry Sauce):

2 cups sugar
2 tablespoons cornstarch
1 cup boiling water
2 cups huckleberry juice

¼ cup sliced almonds

Mix the sugar, salt, and cornstarch or flour thoroughly; stir in the eggs and add scalded milk gradually, stirring until the sugar is dissolved. Cook in a double boiler about 10 to 15 minutes or until the mixture coats a metal spoon; stir constantly during cooking. Remove from the heat; add the flavoring; pour into large serving dish or into individual cups or glasses. Let cool; place in refrigerator to chill.

To make huckleberry sauce: mix the sugar and cornstarch together; stir in the boiling water gradually. Boil for 5 minutes, stirring constantly. Stir in the fruit juice and chill.

Decorate the custard with almonds before serving and serve with the huckleberry sauce. Yield: 6-8 servings.

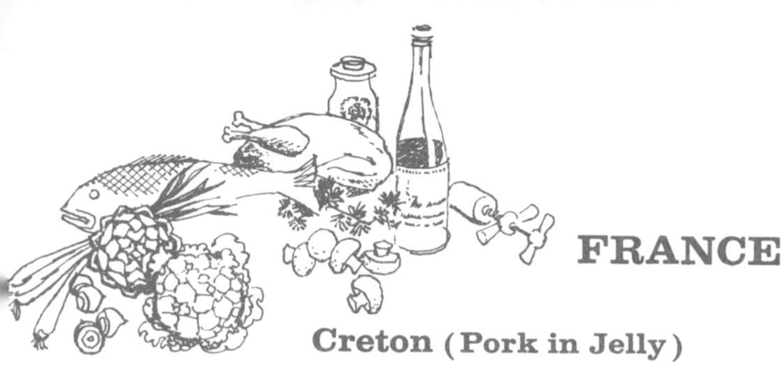

FRANCE

Creton (Pork in Jelly)

3 pounds pork shoulder, ground
2 onions, chopped
1 pig's knuckle or 1 pig's foot
Water
2 teaspoons salt
¼ teaspoon ground black pepper
1 bay leaf
¼ teaspoon thyme
¼ teaspoon basil
1 tablespoon dried parsley or 8 fresh sprigs
¼ teaspoon ground allspice
Garnishes

Place ground pork, onion and pig's knuckle or foot in a large pot and cover with cold water. Add all of the seasonings. Boil for three hours.

Remove knuckle or foot and bay leaf. Dip a mold in cold water and pour mixture into mold. Refrigerate until jellied. Unmold and serve garnished with pickled beets and sliced eggs, or tomatoes and cucumbers, or sliced on French bread as an appetizer. Yield: 8-10 servings.

Seafood Bisque

6 tablespoons butter
6 ounces shrimp, shelled and deveined
6 ounces scallops
3 medium fillets of flounder or sole
1 lobster tail or 1 6-ounce can
3 tablespoons flour
1 cup heavy cream
2½ cups milk
1 teaspoon salt
Few grains pepper
2 teaspoons Worcestershire sauce
1 tablespoon Parmesan cheese
1½ teaspoons capers
½ teaspoon paprika
1 3½-ounce can of crab
3 tablespoons sherry
2 tablespoons chopped parsley

Melt butter in a 12-inch skillet. Cut shrimp, scallops, fillets and lobster (if raw) into bite-size pieces and sauté in butter about 8 minutes, turning once. Remove fish.

Stir flour in remaining fat and add ½ cup of cream; cook over low heat, stirring constantly until a smooth thick paste is formed. Add remaining cream and milk and stir until well combined; add salt, pepper, Worcestershire sauce, cheese, capers, and paprika. Stir well; use a whisk if necessary to make smooth.

Add sautéed fish and crab; heat but do not let boil. Just before serving stir in sherry, and garnish with parsley. Serve hot with French bread. Yield: 6 servings.

Beurre Blanc (Delicate Cream Sauce)

- ½ cup shallots, finely chopped
- ½ tablespoon sweet butter, melted
- 1 cup white wine
- ½ pint heavy cream
- ½ pound sweet butter
- ¼ lemon (optional)

Cook the shallots in ½ tablespoon of butter over low heat. (If mixture should take color, add half a cup of white wine immediately.)

Add the white wine to the mixture, and cook until the mixture is reduced by two-thirds. Add heavy cream and let the mixture reduce again by one-half.

Remove from heat and let stand about 5 minutes. Warm small pieces of butter in your palm and drop in mixture, whipping quickly and strongly until it foams and becomes white. (Add lemon if you wish it a little sour). Yield: 2½ cups.

Crêpes aux Champignons
(Pancakes Stuffed with Mushrooms)

Pancake Batter:

- 4 eggs, well beaten
- 2 cups milk
- 1 tablespoon brandy
- ¼ cup melted butter
- ½ teaspoon salt
- 2 cups flour

Mushroom Stuffing:

- 2 pounds fresh mushrooms, washed and thinly sliced
- ¼ cup melted butter
- ¼ cup flour
- 2 cups chicken stock

- ¼ pound Gruyère cheese, grated

Combine eggs, milk, brandy, butter, and salt; mix thoroughly. Stir in flour; mix until smooth. Let mixture stand while preparing mushroom stuffing. To bake pancakes, preheat lightly greased griddle. For each pancake, pour 2 tablespoons batter onto hot griddle; lightly brown one side. Turn and brown the other side; remove to a baking sheet. Place pancakes on top of each other.

To make stuffing: put mushrooms in melted butter in a large frying pan; cover; cook over low heat until mushrooms are slightly browned and tender; stir and turn occasionally. Sprinkle flour over mushrooms; stir with a fork to coat mushrooms and blend with fat. Add stock gradually, stirring to make smooth mixture. Cook over low heat until mixture is thick. Cool while pancakes are being baked.

Using pancakes cooked first, place about 2 tablespoons mushroom stuffing on each; roll like a jelly roll and place edge-side down on baking sheet. Sprinkle each pancake with cheese; bake at 350°F for 10 minutes before serving. Serve with dry sherry in a cruet or small decanter. Yield: 30 pancakes.

GABON

Poulet au Gnemboue (Chicken with Nuts)

- 1 cup palm or macadamia nuts
- 1¾ cups water
- ½ teaspoon red pepper
- ¼ teaspoon black pepper
- 1 teaspoon salt
- 1 clove garlic
- 3 scallions or green onions, thinly sliced
- 1 2½-pound chicken, cut for frying

Pulverize nuts with mortar and pestle and mix with the water or put nuts in blender with the water. Pour into a 12-inch skillet or sauce pan; stir in the peppers, salt, garlic, and onions; mix ingredients well.

Place pieces of chicken in the nut mixture; cover and cook over very low heat for 1½ hours. Check often; stir and add water if needed. Yield: 4-6 servings.

GHANA

Fante Kotokyim (Crab Sauce)

- 1 small onion, chopped fine
- 3 fresh tomatoes
- ¼ cup butter, melted
- 1 pound crab or lobster meat, fresh, frozen, or canned
- ½ teaspoon ground ginger
- ¼ teaspoon white pepper
- ½ teaspoon salt
- ½ cup water

Cook onion and tomato in melted butter in medium-size frying pan over low heat for 5 minutes. Add bite-sized pieces of crab or lobster meat, ginger, pepper, salt and water; simmer gently for 15 minutes. Serve hot over dry rice or with baked potatoes. Yield: 4 servings.

Fante Mbire Flowee
(Beef and Mushroom Stew)

1½ pounds mushrooms, washed
1½ pounds beef stew meat or pot roast, cut in 1-inch cubes
½ teaspoon salt
¼ teaspoon pepper
6 to 8 tablespoons flour
½ cup vegetable oil
2 small onions, chopped
1 large tomato, chopped
1½ cups water

Cut large mushrooms in quarters; leave button mushrooms whole. Dredge mushrooms and meat in mixture of salt, pepper, and flour. Dip mushrooms in oil; lift from oil and set aside. Brown meat quickly on all sides in hot oil in large frying pan. Remove meat from oil and add onions and tomatoes to same oil; cook until onions are light brown. Add remainder of seasoned flour to onions and stir until mixed. Add water slowly, stirring to produce a smooth sauce. Add mushrooms and meat; stir until well mixed. Cover; simmer for 1 hour, add water if needed during cooking. Serve with rice or mashed potatoes. Yield: 6 servings.

GREECE

Fish à la Spetsiota (Baked Red Snapper)

2 pounds red snapper fillets
2 teaspoons salt
¼ teaspoon pepper
2 tablespoons lemon juice
2 cups canned tomatoes, drained
½ cup white wine
⅓ cup olive oil
½ cup minced parsley
2 cloves garlic, crushed
⅓ cup dry bread crumbs
½ cup tomato juice

Cut ready-to-cook red snapper into 12 pieces; rub with salt and pepper. Combine all other ingredients except bread crumbs and tomato juice; pour into a casserole or baking dish. Place fish in sauce. Cover with bread crumbs; pour tomato juice into the casserole near the edge. Bake uncovered in a 350°F oven for 1½ hours. Yield: 6 servings.

Riganato (Lamb Oregano)

- 2 pounds leg of lamb
- 1½ teaspoons salt
- ⅛ teaspoon pepper
- 1 clove garlic, cut into eighths
- ⅓ cup cooking oil
- 2 tablespoons lemon juice
- 2 cups hot water
- 1 teaspoon oregano
- 1½ pounds small potatoes, peeled

Rub lamb with salt and pepper; insert garlic in slits or pockets made in lamb with sharp knife. Brown lamb in hot fat in Dutch oven or deep skillet (with tight fitting cover). Add lemon juice and 1½ cups hot water; cover and cook over simmering heat for 1 hour. Add oregano and cook for 30 minutes; uncover and allow liquid to evaporate. Increase heat; add potatoes; brown, turning often. When potatoes are brown, reduce heat; add remaining water. Cover and continue cooking over low heat for 30 minutes or until potatoes are done. Yield: 6 servings.

Loukoumades (Cinnamon Fritters)

- 1 package of yeast
- ½ cup lukewarm water
- ½ cup scalded milk
- 1 egg, well beaten
- 2 cups flour
- 1½ teaspoons baking powder
- ¼ teaspoon salt
- 1 quart vegetable oil for deep-fat frying
- 1 teaspoon cinnamon

Syrup:

- 1 cup sugar
- ½ cup honey
- ¾ cup water

Combine yeast and warm water in a medium sized mixing bowl; add milk which has cooled to lukewarm, and egg. Add flour sifted with baking powder and salt to the yeast mixture. Beat thoroughly until batter is free of lumps. Cover and let rise in warm, draft-free place until double in size.

Heat oil in deep-fat fryer or heavy sauce pan to 350°F. Drop the batter by teaspoonful into the hot fat, using a spatula to help regulate the size of the fritter. Brown on both sides; remove from fat and drain on absorbent paper. Sprinkle with cinnamon while hot and serve with hot syrup as a dessert.

To make syrup: combine sugar, honey, and water and boil for 5 minutes.

Yield: 25 fritters.

GUATEMALA

Chiles Rellenos (Fried Green Peppers)

- 6 large green peppers
- 1 large tomato, chopped
- ½ cup minced onion
- 1 teaspoon salt
- ¼ teaspoon black pepper
- Few grains cayenne pepper
- ⅔ pound ground beef
- 1 quart cooking oil for frying
- 1 cup cooked rice
- 2 eggs
- 2 tablespoons milk
- 2 tablespoons flour

Cut tops from peppers; remove seeds and wash well. Save the tops. Place peppers under the broiler for about 5 minutes or long enough to soften slightly.

Combine tomato, onion, salt, and peppers; cook until onion is soft.

Cook ground meat in a skillet with 2 tablespoons of oil until seared but not browned, separating with a fork. Remove meat to absorbent paper to take up extra fat. Start heating oil for deep-fat frying in a 2½ to 3-quart saucepan. Combine tomato mixture, ground meat, and cooked rice. Fill pepper cups with mixture. Replace pepper tops and tie securely with twine. Combine eggs, milk, and flour. Dip the stuffed peppers, one at a time, in the batter.

Fat should be heated to 390°F, and a deep-fry pan with basket used. Place 3 peppers at a time in the basket; immerse in hot fat and fry until pepper is golden brown. Remove; drain and keep in a warm place until all peppers are cooked. Serve with a thin tomato sauce. Yield: 6 servings.

Arroz con Pollo (Chicken with Rice)

- ½ cup vegetable oil
- 1 3-pound frying chicken or 2½ pounds chicken breasts, legs and thighs
- 4 ounces smoked ham, cut in small pieces (hocks may be used)
- 1 medium green pepper, chopped
- 4-6 stuffed green olives, chopped
- 1 large tomato, cut in small pieces
- 2 small onions, quartered
- 2 cloves garlic
- 1 teaspoon capers
- ¼ teaspoon powdered oregano
- 2 teaspoons salt
- ¼ teaspoon pepper
- 1¼ cups rice
- 3 cups water

Heat oil in Dutch oven or 12-inch frying pan and brown chicken; add all other ingredients except the rice and water. Cover; cook slowly until chicken is almost tender; then, add rice and water. Cover and cook until rice is done and water absorbed. Yield: 6 servings.

GUINEA

Kansiyé (Guinean Goulash)

- 1 pound beef, lamb, or a small chicken
- 3 tablespoons oil
- 1 large onion, chopped
- ½ teaspoon salt
- ⅛ teaspoon pepper
- ⅛ teaspoon thyme
- 2 cloves garlic, minced
- 1 tablespoon minced parsley
- 1 whole clove, ground
- 1 6-ounce can tomato sauce
- 3 cups water
- 3 tablespoons smooth peanut butter

Cut beef or lamb into 1-inch cubes; if chicken is used, cut in serving pieces. Brown meat in oil in 10-inch frying pan. Add onion, salt, pepper, thyme, garlic, parsley, and cloves. Combine tomato sauce and 2 cups water; add to seasoned meat and mix well. Dilute peanut butter with 1 cup water and add to mixture. Cook over medium heat for 1 hour or until meat is tender. (Small chicken may cook more quickly than beef or lamb; amount of water may be reduced to 2½ cups). Serve hot over rice. Yield: 4-6 servings.

HAITI

Tassau (Veal Cutlets)

12 veal cutlets, thinly sliced
1 cup boiled water
1/4 teaspoon garlic powder
1/8 teaspoon thyme powder
1 tablespoon dried parsley flakes
1/8 teaspoon pepper
1 teaspoon sugar
1/2 teaspoon salt
1/2 cup orange juice
1/2 cup lemonade
4 tablespoons vegetable oil

Beat cutlets with meat hammer. Add cutlets to boiled water which should still be warm. Mix garlic powder, thyme, parsley flakes, pepper, sugar and salt with orange juice; stir this mixture and lemonade into the cutlets and water mixture. Cover; place in refrigerator for at least 4 hours. Remove cutlets; drain and brown in hot oil in heavy frying pan. Marinade sauce can be poured into frying pan and placed over low heat; loosen browned bits adhering to pan. Serve as a sauce with the cutlets. Yield: 6 servings.

Soupe au Giraumon (Vegetable Soup)

1 pound chicken breasts
1 1-pound ham hock
1 cup orange juice
2 teaspoons salt
1/2 pound summer squash, sliced
2 carrots, sliced
1 small head cabbage, shredded
1 rib celery, sliced
1 cup rice
1 onion, sliced and cooked in 1 tablespoon butter
3 cloves
1 tablespoon cider vinegar
1/2 pound spaghetti, broken in 2-inch lengths

Soak chicken and ham in orange juice for 1 hour; turn often. Rub chicken and ham with salt; place in a 5-quart soup kettle; fill with water to within 1-inch of top. Bring to a boil and simmer 2½ to 3 hours; skim top. Add squash, carrots, cabbage, celery, and rice; simmer about 25 minutes or until vegetables are tender.

Remove meat; strain vegetables from liquid and return liquid to kettle. Add water to liquid to make 3 quarts; bring to a boil; add cooked onions, cloves, vinegar, and spaghetti. Boil for about 10 minutes or until spaghetti is done. Taste for seasoning and correct, if necessary. Serve the meat and vegetables as a separate course from the soup or return to the soup after the spaghetti is tender and serve as a stew. Yield: 6 to 8 servings.

Aubergines en Peau (Cheese Stuffed Eggplant)

- 1 eggplant, cut in half, lengthwise
- Water
- 2 tablespoons diced onion
- 2 teaspoons butter
- 2 slices stale bread soaked in ½ cup milk — squeezed dry
- 2 tablespoons condensed cream of chicken soup
- Salt and pepper
- 1 egg, lightly beaten
- 6 tablespoons grated Cheddar cheese
- ½ cup buttered bread crumbs

Boil eggplant in water to cover for 3 minutes. Drain, remove pulp and dice, leaving enough pulp to have firm shell. Cook onion and eggplant in hot fat for 5 minutes; add bread, chicken soup, salt, and pepper and continue cooking for 5 minutes. Remove from heat; stir in egg and 3 tablespoons of the cheese. Fill the eggplant shells with the mixture; sprinkle with remaining cheese and bread crumbs. Place filled shells in greased casserole and bake for 25 minutes in 350°F oven. Yield: 4 to 6 servings.

HONDURAS

Arroz con Pollo (Chicken with Rice)

- 1 3-pound chicken, quartered
- 1 teaspoon salt
- 2 cups water
- 1 large onion, quartered
- 1 clove garlic, minced
- 1 teaspoon caraway seeds
- ½ cup tomato paste
- 1 cup rice
- 2 tablespoons oil
- 1 cup pitted black olives, sliced
- 1 cup canned peas
- 1 carrot, diced
- 1 cup beer or white wine
- 2 cups finely shredded cabbage
- ½ cup capers

Cook chicken in salted water with onion, garlic, caraway seeds, and tomato paste until chicken is tender, about 45 minutes. Remove chicken from broth and cool; skin, bone, and mince chicken. Fry rice in hot oil in heavy saucepan until golden brown; add chicken, broth, olives, peas, and carrot. Add beer or white wine to cover mixture; bring to boil and simmer until rice is almost done. Add the cabbage and capers; continue simmering for 10 minutes. Yield: 6 to 8 servings.

Potato-Tuna Fish Salad

- 2 cups finely shredded cabbage or lettuce
- 6 medium potatoes, cooked and diced
- 1 1-pound can peas
- 1 small onion, grated
- 1 teaspoon salt
- ½ teaspoon pepper
- 1 cup mayonnaise
- 2 tablespoons lemon juice
- 1 7-ounce can tuna fish, drained

Place cabbage in large serving bowl; spread to line bottom and sides of bowl.

Combine potatoes, peas, onion, salt, and pepper in mixing bowl; fold in mayonnaise and lemon juice. Turn this mixture on the bed of cabbage; dot surface with flakes of tuna. Yield: 8 to 10 servings.

Note: An additional can of tuna fish may be combined with vegetables and mayonnaise.

HUNGARY

Bouillon

- ½ pound lean beef, minced
- 1 egg white
- 2 tablespoons tomato purée
- 8 cups cold water
- 1 pound beef bones
- 3 small carrots, diced
- 1 large parsnip, diced
- 3 stalks celery, diced
- 2 small kohlrabi or turnips, diced
- ⅓ cup savoy or white cabbage, shredded
- 1 small onion, diced
- 2 large mushrooms, sliced
- 1 small green pepper, diced
- 1 clove garlic
- 5 whole peppercorns
- 2 tablespoons salt

Put beef, egg white, and tomato purée in large Dutch oven or saucepan and mix well. Add water and stir until mixed. Add beef bones, vegetables, and seasonings. Cover and simmer for 4 hours. Strain and serve hot. Yield: 5 pints or 10 servings.

Szekely Gulyas

(Pork and Sauerkraut Stew)

- 1 pound pork, shoulder
- 1 pound ribs of pork
- 3 large onions, chopped
- 2 tablespoons lard or other fat
- 2 cloves garlic, crushed
- ½ teaspoon caraway seeds
- ½ teaspoon paprika
- 1 cup water
- 1 teaspoon salt
- 2 pounds sauerkraut
- 2 teaspoons flour
- 1 pint sour cream

Cut meat and ribs in 2-inch pieces. Cook onions in fat in Dutch oven or 12-inch frying pan until yellow. Add garlic, caraway seeds, paprika, and water; bring to a boil. Add meat, ribs, and salt. Cover, and simmer for 1 hour. Add sauerkraut and enough water to cover. Cook about 45 minutes or until meat is tender; stir occasionally. Blend flour and sour cream; add to the stew and simmer for 5 minutes. Serve with buttered noodles. Yield: 8 servings.

Chocolate Mignons

- ¼ cup butter
- ½ cup sugar
- 4 eggs, separated
- 2 squares (2 ounces) unsweetened chocolate
- 1 tablespoon cocoa
- ¼ cup flour, sifted
- 2 tablespoons almonds, finely ground

Filling:

- ½ cup apricot or other jam
- 2 tablespoons rum

Mocha Frosting:

- 4 tablespoons butter
- ½ tablespoon cocoa
- 1¾ cups confectioners' sugar
- 2 tablespoons strong coffee
- ½ teaspoon vanilla

Cream butter with ¼ cup sugar until fluffy. Add the egg yolks, one by one, beating well after each addition. Melt the chocolate, blend in cocoa and add to egg and butter mixture, beating well. Beat the egg whites until stiff and gradually fold the remaining ¼ cup of sugar into the egg whites. Fold egg whites into chocolate mixture and blend in flour and almonds. Pour into an oiled and floured 8-inch cake pan or an oblong pan. Bake at 350°F for 20 to 25 minutes or until done. When done, invert over cake rack and cool.

To make filling: mix jam and rum. Cut cake into two thin layers, and spread top of bottom layer with filling. Replace top layer. Cut cake in 2-inch squares.

To make Mocha Frosting: cream the butter; add combined mixture of cocoa and sugar gradually alternating with coffee. Add vanilla and blend until creamy. Spread tops and sides of cake squares with the frosting. Yield: 16 2-inch squares.

ICELAND

Kjötbögglar (Meat Rolls in Cabbage Leaves)

- 1 large head cabbage, green
- Boiling water
- 1½ pounds ground lean beef
- ½ cup flour
- ¼ cup cornstarch
- 1 onion, diced fine
- ¼ cup butter
- 1 cup milk
- 1 tablespoon salt
- ½ teaspoon pepper
- 3 eggs, beaten

Cook whole cabbage head for 10 minutes in large kettle of boiling water. Remove from water, drain, and cool. Cut and separate outer leaves from cabbage, about 12 leaves. Combine remaining ingredients and mix well. Place 1 to 2 tablespoons of meat mixture on each cabbage leaf. Fold leaf around meat and secure with toothpicks. Place stuffed leaves in kettle with the remainder of the cabbage; boil gently for ½ hour. Serve with boiled potatoes which may be boiled with meat rolls and cabbage, or separately. Yield: 6 servings.

Fiskibudingur (Fish Soufflé)

- 1 pound fish, cod, haddock, or red snapper
- Water
- ½ cup butter or margarine
- 1 cup sifted flour
- 1¼ cups milk
- 1 teaspoon salt
- Few grains of pepper
- 6 eggs, yolks and whites separated
- 1 tablespoon soft butter
- ½ cup bread crumbs

Simmer the fish in a small amount of water until tender; remove skin and bones; break into rather thick flakes.

Melt the butter or margarine in a sauce pan; add flour and stir until smooth. Add milk and cook until very thick. Season with salt and pepper. Cool sauce; add egg yolks and beat well; combine the fish and sauce; fold the beaten egg whites into the fish mixture. Pour mixture into a buttered 2-quart casserole coated with crumbs. Sprinkle bread crumbs over the top and bake in 375°F oven for 55 minutes. Yield: 6-8 servings.

Note: 1-inch thick slices of cold, left-over soufflé may be sautéed in butter and served for breakfast.

Eplakaka (Apple Cake)

- 2 cups soft bread crumbs
- ¾ cup sugar
- ½ cup butter
- 2 cups applesauce
- ½ cup fruit or berry jam (optional)
- ½ cup heavy cream, whipped

Combine breadcrumbs and sugar; sauté in butter slowly until browned. Place alternate layers of breadcrumbs and applesauce in glass bowl or serving dish. A thin layer of jam may be used between layers or on top as desired. Serve warm or chilled with whipped cream sweetened to taste. Yield: 6 servings.

INDIA

Shrimp Bhaji (Curried Shrimp)

2 medium onions, ground
1 teaspoon crushed garlic
¼ cup peanut oil
½ teaspoon crushed ginger root or ¼ teaspoon ground ginger
1 cup chopped fresh tomato
1 teaspoon vinegar
1 teaspoon salt
½ teaspoon chili powder
1 teaspoon curry powder
⅛ teaspoon turmeric
½ cup water
2 pounds cooked shrimp, deveined and cut in ½-inch pieces

Combine onions and garlic; cook in hot peanut oil until onions and garlic are golden brown. Stir the ginger, tomato, vinegar, salt, chili powder, curry powder, turmeric and water into the onion and garlic mixture. Stir only until blended; cover and simmer sauce for 10 minutes or until mixture is slightly thickened. Add shrimp to sauce; simmer for 15 minutes. Serve with dry rice. Yield: 6 servings.

Masala Machali (Stuffed Fish)

½ cup fresh or canned coconut
½ teaspoon crushed ginger root or ¼ teaspoon ground ginger
½ cup finely chopped mint leaves
2 tablespoons milk
2 tablespoons lemon juice
½ teaspoon curry powder
½ teaspoon red pepper
1 teaspoon salt
3 pounds flounder or sole fillets
1 lemon
2 to 3 cups peanut oil for deep-fat frying
½ cup chopped onions cooked in 2 tablespoons butter

Grind coconut and ginger root, using fine blade. Combine with mint, milk, lemon juice, curry powder, red pepper, and salt to form a paste. Wash and dry fish; cut slit or pocket in each fillet; rub well with lemon. Fill pockets with paste mixture; secure with thread. Deep-fat fry the fish in hot oil until brown and done but not overcooked. Remove from fat; drain on absorbent paper; garnish with cooked onions. Yield: 6 servings.

Benegal Fish Curry

2 dried chili peppers, finely crushed
1 teaspoon turmeric
1 teaspoon salt
2 pounds halibut steak, cut in 1-inch cubes
3 tablespoons vegetable oil

Curry Sauce:

1 teaspoon coriander seeds
1 teaspoon cardamon seeds
1 teaspoon cumin seeds
2 teaspoons mustard seeds
2 pounds onions
1 teaspoon turmeric
½ teaspoon cinnamon
½ teaspoon chili powder
1 teaspoon salt
4 cloves garlic
¼ cup vegetable oil
1 pound tomatoes, peeled and sliced
1 cup yogurt

Mix crushed chili peppers, turmeric and salt together. Sprinkle over halibut cubes and coat well. Heat oil in large frying pan and brown the fish on all sides. Remove fish from pan, drain, and set aside.

To make Curry Sauce: grind together coriander, cardamon, cumin, and mustard seeds, with ½ of the onions. Add the turmeric, cinnamon, chili powder and salt to the ground onion and spice mixture. Slice remaining half of onions. Cook sliced onions and garlic in oil in frying pan until brown. Add the ground onion and spice mixture, and sliced tomatoes, to the browned onions and garlic. Cook gently until tomatoes are tender. Add well-beaten yogurt and cook over medium heat for 5 minutes.

Add fried fish to curry sauce and simmer for 10 minutes. Remove garlic. Serve hot with a tomato chutney. Yield: 6 servings.

Chicken Curry

⅓ cup vegetable shortening
2 medium onions, sliced thin
2-3 cloves garlic, minced
1 teaspoon powdered ginger
1-3 tablespoons curry powder
1 tablespoon chili powder
1 large frying chicken, disjointed
1 cup chicken stock
1 tomato, sliced
1 cup cottage cheese, small curd
Salt to taste

Heat fat and fry onions, garlic, ginger, curry powder, and chili powder until lightly browned. Add chicken pieces, cover, and continue cooking for 15 minutes. Stir in remaining ingredients, cover, and simmer until chicken is tender, about 40 minutes. Serve with rice. Yield: 6 servings.

IRAN

Khoreshe Karafs (Beef-Celery Sauce)

- 1 large onion, finely chopped
- 2 tablespoons butter
- 1½ pounds tender beef
- 1 teaspoon salt
- ½ teaspoon pepper
- 1 teaspoon cinnamon
- ½ teaspoon nutmeg
- ¾ cup water
- 2 tablespoons butter
- 4 cups diced celery
- 1 cup chopped parsley
- 3 tablespoons lemon juice

Cook onion in butter in large frying pan until yellow. Remove onion from fat. Add beef, salt, pepper, cinnamon and nutmeg to fat and cook over low heat until meat is brown. Add water and cooked onions; cover and simmer until meat is tender.

Melt butter in another large frying pan and sauté celery and parsley for 10 minutes. Add celery and parsley mixture and lemon juice to the beef mixture and simmer for 15 minutes. Serve with Chelo or steamed rice. Yield: 6 servings.

Paludeh Seeb (Apple Delight Dessert)

- 4 medium apples
- 2 tablespoons lemon juice
- 4 to 6 tablespoons powdered sugar
- 2 teaspoons rosewater
- 3 ice cubes

Pare and grate apples, and add to lemon juice. Add sugar and rosewater. Stir lightly. Add ice cubes, which serve to chill and dilute the mixture. Yield: 4 servings.

Chelo (Golden Rice)

- 1⅓ cups long-grain white rice
- 2 teaspoons salt
- 1 quart water
- ¼ cup melted butter
- 1 tablespoon water

Add rice and salt to boiling water. Stir, cover, and reduce to low heat. Cook for 15 minutes; drain in colander or sieve and rinse with lukewarm water. Place half of the melted butter in a Dutch oven or similarly heavy pan with a lid. Add the tablespoon of water and spoon rice over bottom of pan and pile up in the shape of a cone. Pour remainder of melted butter over the rice. Place several layers of paper toweling over the top of the cooking utensil and cover with tight fitting lid. Cook for 10 to 15 minutes over medium heat in order for rice to form a crisp, golden brown crust on the bottom of the pan. Reduce heat and simmer for 35 to 40 minutes. More butter may be added before serving. Yield: 6 servings.

Morg Polo (Chicken with Golden Rice)

- 1 recipe of Chelo
- 1 large onion, finely chopped
- 5 tablespoons butter
- 1 teaspoon poultry seasoning
- ¼ teaspoon cinnamon
- 1 teaspoon salt
- ¼ teaspoon pepper
- 3 pounds choice pieces of chicken
- ⅔ cup seedless raisins
- ½ cup dried apricots, chopped
- 1½ tablespoons butter

Begin preparation of Chelo (see previous recipe). Cook chopped onion in butter until golden; remove onion. Mix poultry seasoning, cinnamon, salt, and pepper, and sprinkle over chicken. Brown seasoned chicken in fat remaining from cooking onions.

Wash raisins and chopped apricots and soak in cold water to cover for 5 minutes. Drain well, and cook over low heat in butter for 5 minutes. When Chelo is ready to be placed in butter in heavy pan, proceed according to directions until half of rice has been placed in pan. Arrange chicken, onions, and dried fruit over rice. Place remaining half of rice on top of mound and add butter as directed for Chelo. Cover top of utensil with paper toweling and with close fitting lid. Follow directions for cooking Chelo. Yield: 6 servings.

IRAQ

Kubba Shalgum

(Turnip Soup with Meat Balls)

5 turnips, peeled, and sliced
1 large onion, chopped
2 tablespoons fat
8 cups water
1½ teaspoons salt
4 tablespoons tomato paste
2 pounds lean ground beef
1 cup cream of rice, uncooked
Water
1½ pounds ground lamb shoulder
1 cup minced onion
¼ cup minced parsley
1 tablespoon fat
½ cup raisins
½ cup blanched almonds, sliced
2 tablespoons cream of rice, uncooked
⅓ cup lemon juice
6 spinach leaves or sprigs of parsley

Cook turnips and onion in hot fat in large heavy kettle or Dutch oven until onions are yellow. Add the water, salt, and tomato paste; bring to a boil and boil for 15 minutes. Reduce heat and simmer for 30 minutes.

Combine the beef, cream of rice, and sufficient water to mold mixture with your hands. Set aside.

Mix the lamb, minced onion, and parsley; cook in 1 tablespoon of fat until meat is brown and thoroughly cooked. Add raisins and almonds.

Divide the mixture of beef and cream of rice into four equal portions; divide each of these into 6 equal portions. Flatten each portion into about a 3-inch round or patty. Place 1 teaspoon of lamb mixture in the center of patty. Shape into a round ball, keeping the lamb within the beef-rice mixture.

Add the 2 tablespoons of uncooked cream of rice, lemon juice, and spinach leaves or sprigs of parsley to the soup. Bring soup to simmering point; drop meat balls into the soup and simmer uncovered for 25 minutes. Serve soup with meat balls while piping hot. Yield: 8 servings.

Bulgar (Cracked Wheat)

1 pound bulgar
3½ cups water
¼ pound butter or margarine
1 teaspoon salt
2 eggplants, medium size
1 onion, chopped
2 tablespoons fat
½ cup chopped parsley

Wash the bulgar with cold water in a sieve. Bring the 3½ cups of water to boiling point and add fat and salt. Slowly add the bulgar. Boil until most of the water is absorbed; cover and simmer slowly for 1 hour.

Peel the eggplants; cut into 1½-inch squares. Cook eggplants and onion in the 2 tablespoons of fat until done.

Add the parsley to the eggplant and onion mixture; fold into the hot bulgar and serve as vegetable. Yield: 8 servings.

Note: Bulgar, a staple food in the Middle East, available in parts of the U.S. as Redi-Wheat and as cracked wheat bulgar. Used in the same way as rice.

IRELAND

Sole Atchen (Stuffed Fillet of Sole Supreme)

¾ cup fresh mushrooms
2 teaspoons chives
¼ cup fennel, chopped
½ cup butter
¼ teaspoon salt
6 cooked shrimp, chopped
½ cup heavy cream
2 pounds sole fillets

Cook mushrooms, chives, and fennel in hot butter until mushrooms are done; add salt and shrimp. Continue cooking for 5 minutes; add cream; reduce heat and stir. Cream should be absorbed.

Place ½ of fillets in a shallow, greased baking dish; place stuffing on each fillet, then place a matching fillet on top of stuffing. Bake at 375°F for 25 to 30 minutes. Yield: 6 servings.

Queen Cakes

¾ cup margarine
1 cup superfine granulated sugar
3 large eggs, well beaten
3 cups sifted flour
2 teaspoons baking powder

Cream margarine and sugar. Stir in eggs and beat for 5 minutes. Sift flour and baking powder; add slowly to creamed mixture, mixing well after each addition. Fill cups of greased muffin pans one-half full. Bake at 375°F for 20 to 25 minutes, according to size of muffin cups. Yield: 18 cup cakes.

Curaimir (Venison Cutlets)

- 2½ pounds venison cutlets
- 1 pint elderberry wine
- 4 tablespoons butter
- 3 tomatoes
- ½ pound mushrooms

Marinate venison in wine overnight or at least for 3 hours. Drain and pan-fry in hot butter until meat is tender and brown. Remove meat to serving platter; add ½ cup of wine used for marinating to pan in which cutlets were cooked. Simmer to loosen bits of browned meat adhering to pan and pour hot sauce over cutlets.

Cut tomatoes in halves; dredge in seasoned flour (¼ cup flour, ½ teaspoon salt, and ¼ teaspoon pepper); arrange on a greased shallow pan with mushrooms. Place under broiler until surface is brown; then in hot oven for 3 to 5 minutes to complete cooking. Serve with venison. Yield: 6 servings.

Baked Stuffed Duckling Cathal

Stuffing:

- 4 large cooking apples, peeled and quartered
- ¼ cup margarine
- 1 cup cider
- 1 teaspoon salt
- ¼ teaspoon pepper
- ¼ teaspoon nutmeg
- 1 teaspoon chopped parsley
- ½ teaspoon fennel seeds
- 1 teaspoon chopped mint
- 5 slices day-old bread

- 4 to 5 pound roaster duckling, pan ready
- ½ cup flour
- 1 teaspoon salt
- 4 tablespoons margarine
- 2 large onions, sliced
- ¼ teaspoon ground cloves
- 1 cup apple cider
- 1 bay leaf
- 2 apples, cored and sliced
- 1 tablespoon cornstarch
- 2 tablespoons cold water

To make stuffing: cook apples in melted fat over low heat until tender and slightly browned. Add cider and cook gently for 10 minutes. (Apple pieces should hold their shape.) Fold in seasonings and bread broken into small pieces. Liquid should be absorbed.

Stuff duckling, truss, and dredge with flour and salt. Melt margarine in lower section of roasting pan and brown duckling on all sides. When almost browned, add onions and cook until yellow or transparent. Add cloves, cider, and bay leaf. Place duckling breast side up on rack in roasting pan. Pour cider and onions over duckling. Cover; bake at 350°F for 2 hours. Place apple slices around duckling during last 20 minutes of baking. Remove duckling to serving platter; garnish with apple slices; keep warm. Strain remaining liquid into small saucepan. Add paste made from cornstarch and cold water. Simmer for 5 minutes. Skim off fat before serving. Serve with rice cooked in orange juice; garnish with chopped walnuts. Yield: 6 servings.

ISRAEL

Chocolate Date Nut Pie

1 8-ounce package pitted dates
Boiling water
4 ounces milk chocolate
2 tablespoons margarine
1 10-ounce angel food cake, broken into small pieces
½ cup chopped nuts
1 pint heavy cream
1 tablespoon sugar
1 tablespoon cocoa
1 tablespoon instant coffee
Chocolate for topping

Soak dates in boiling water for 5 minutes; remove from water and mash. Melt chocolate and margarine over hot water; stir into the dates. Fold angel food cake and nuts into chocolate mixture; pour into 9-inch pie pan; and refrigerate.

Mix 1 cup cream, sugar, cocoa, coffee; bring to a boil. Cool and refrigerate. On next day, whip cream mixture until stiff, spread over top of pie. Whip remaining cup of cream and spread over boiled cream mixture. Grate chocolate over top. Yield: 6-8 servings.

Boureka (Meat Squares)

3 cups flour
1 teaspoon salt
½ pound margarine
2 tablespoons oil
½ cup water

Filling:
1 onion, finely diced
2 tablespoons oil
1 pound ground lean hamburger
¼ teaspoon pepper
1 teaspoon salt
½ teaspoon allspice
2 tablespoons chopped parsley
2 tomatoes, peeled and diced
½ cup nuts, ground or finely chopped

1 egg, beaten
½ cup sesame seeds

Blend flour, salt, and margarine together until mixture is similar to cornmeal; mix in oil and water; form dough into a ball. Place on wooden board; cover with a bowl; set aside for 2 to 3 hours. Divide dough in half; roll first half out on a cooky sheet into a 12-inch square.

To make filling: sauté onion in hot oil in a 10-inch frying pan until onion is limp. Add meat and all other ingredients listed except the nuts; cook until meat is thoroughly done and dry. Drain off all excess fat. Stir nuts into meat mixture; cool.

Spread filling evenly over the rolled square. Roll second half into a 12-inch square; place carefully on top of filling and press down gently. Brush top with egg; sprinkle with sesame seeds and cut into 36 squares. Bake in 350°F oven for 30 minutes or until top is brown: Yield 36 2-inch squares or appetizers.

Orange Peel Confections

1 dozen medium oranges, halved and juiced
Water
4 cups sugar (approximately)
¾ pound ground walnuts
1 7-ounce package coconut

Cut the orange halves into eighths. Put in a 5-quart sauce pan and cover with water. Bring to a boil, remove from stove, drain and refill with cold water. Let oranges stand in water for 24 hours changing water at least six times or until peel has lost bitter taste. Drain and put through a grinder. Drain again.

Measure ground orange peel and return to sauce pan. Add an equal amount of sugar and mix well. Cook on low heat, stirring frequently, until mixture reaches a thick jelly consistency. Remove from stove and cool. (At this point the mixture may be stored in covered jars in the refrigerator for a period of several weeks.)

To this mixture add approximately ¾ of ground nuts and ¾ of coconut, depending on the size of your oranges. This is a very stiff mixture and if this cannot be done by electric mixer then knead by hand. Form into balls. Roll balls in remaining nuts or coconut. Serve or store in airtight container. Yield: 60 balls.

ITALY

Gnocchi Leggeri (Cheese Noodles) Lazio

1 cup plus 2 tablespoons butter
4 egg yolks
1⅓ cups flour
½ pound grated Parmesan cheese
⅛ teaspoon grated nutmeg
2 teaspoons salt
⅛ teaspoon pepper
4 egg whites, beaten stiff
Melted butter

Cream butter with egg yolks, adding one at a time, until mixture is well blended. Add flour, half of grated cheese, nutmeg, salt and pepper; blend well. Add egg whites and refrigerate mixture thoroughly.

Toss on slightly floured board and roll to ¼ inch thick; cut in 1-inch strips and again to form small cubes. Boil in salted water until noodles float. Drain well; alternate layers of noodles, Parmesan cheese, and melted butter in serving dish. Yield: 6 servings.

Stracciatella (Chicken Soup with Egg Drops)

2 quarts cold water
2 pounds chicken wings, necks, and backs
1 rib celery with leaves, sliced
2 carrots, sliced
1 small onion, diced
1 teaspoon salt
½ teaspoon pepper
4 eggs, beaten
½ - 1 cup Parmesan cheese, grated
1 tablespoon chopped parsley
Salt and pepper to taste

Place chicken in large kettle with water. Cover and bring to a boil. Skim surface; add celery, carrots, onion, salt, and pepper. Cover; cook slowly until meat is very tender. Strain broth into saucepan and keep hot.

Combine eggs, cheese, and parsley. Bring 7 cups of chicken broth to the boiling point, and gradually pour egg mixture into broth, stirring constantly with a fork or wooden spoon to prevent lumping. Simmer about 5 minutes until egg drops are cooked. Add salt and pepper if needed. Serve hot. Yield: 6 servings.

Funghi Ripieni (Stuffed Mushrooms)

12 large mushrooms, fresh
1 cup bread crumbs
½ teaspoon salt
¼ teaspoon pepper
2 tablespoons parsley
1 clove garlic, minced
Chicken bouillon to moisten
2 tablespoons olive oil
½ cup white cooking wine

Cut off and chop stems of mushrooms. Combine bread crumbs, chopped stems, and seasonings. Add bouillon to moisten. Stuff mushroom caps with mixture; brush caps with oil; place in flat oven-proof dish. Pour wine in dish; bake in 350°F for about 30 minutes. Baste several times, using additional bouillon or wine if needed. Yield: 6 appetizers.

Involtini (Rolled Veal with Pâté)

2 pounds veal cutlets, cut very thin
1 teaspoon rosemary
½ cup flour
½ cup grated Parmesan cheese
1 teaspoon salt
¼ teaspoon pepper
1 4-ounce can pâté de foie gras
2 tablespoons butter
1 tablespoon chopped parsley
2 tablespoons oil
1 cup Marsala or dry white wine

Sprinkle each slice of veal with rosemary and pound steak with meat mallet or edge of saucer. Roll meat in mixture of flour, cheese, salt, and pepper; pound both sides of meat again.

Combine pâté de foie gras, butter, and parsley; spread the paste thinly on one side of each piece of meat. Roll each piece tightly (with paste inside) and secure with toothpicks. Sauté gently in oil for 5 to 10 minutes or until veal is brown. Add the wine and simmer for 5 minutes or until rolls are tender. Serve with rice or sliced cold as an appetizer. Yield: 12 appetizers.

IVORY COAST

Chicken à la N'Gatietro
(Fried Chicken with Peanut Butter Sauce)

1 2½ to 3-pound frying chicken, cut for frying
3 tablespoons cooking oil
½ cup chopped onion
3 green onions, sliced
1 large tomato, diced
1 tablespoon tomato paste
1 teaspoon salt
1 teaspoon paprika
1 bay leaf
2 cups water
1 cup peanut butter

Brown chicken in hot oil in frying pan or Dutch oven. Add onions, tomato, tomato paste, salt, paprika, and bay leaf to browned chicken. Cover; cook over low heat for 5 to 10 minutes. Add water to chicken and simmer until chicken is nearly tender. Remove chicken mixture from heat.

Cream peanut butter and chicken stock in mixing bowl; add stock until peanut butter is a light, creamy smooth sauce. Pour sauce over chicken; cover and cook over low heat for about 10 minutes or until chicken is tender. Yield: 6 servings.

JAMAICA

Sweet Potato Pudding

1 pound sweet potatoes, peeled and grated
¼ cup butter, melted
¾ cup brown sugar
¼ cup flour
¼ teaspoon nutmeg
¼ teaspoon ground ginger
⅛ teaspoon salt
2 cups coconut milk (page 27)
½ teaspoon vanilla
½ cup raisins

Combine grated sweet potatoes with butter and sugar. Sift flour with nutmeg, ginger and salt, and add to potato mixture. Add 1 cup of coconut milk slowly; add vanilla and raisins. Pour mixture into oiled baking dish and bake in 375°F oven for 1½ hours or until pudding is firm to touch. Serve as dessert warm or cold with remaining cup of coconut milk. Yield: 6 servings.

JAPAN

Yosenabe (Chicken with Dashi Sauce)

2 chicken breasts, cut in 12 pieces
12 shrimp
12 oysters
12 clams
12 scallops
12 pieces of lobster
1 package frozen spinach
12 strips Chinese cabbage
1 teaspoon monosodium glutamate
1½ cups cooked vermicelli
12 small mushrooms
12 ginko nuts or canned water chestnuts
12 slices bamboo shoots, canned
12 slices carrots

Dashi Sauce:

7 cups water
¾ cup bonito flakes
¾ cup Japanese Soy Sauce
¾ cup sherry

Place all ingredients in a 12-inch skillet or heavy frying pan with the spinach, cabbage, and carrots in the center, and all other ingredients surrounding the vegetables. In so far as possible, keep all of each kind of food together, since each serving usually consists of some of each kind of food used.

To make Dashi Sauce: combine water and bonito flakes and boil for 3 minutes. Strain and discard the flakes. Combine strained liquid (known as Dashi), soy sauce, and sherry.

Pour Dashi Sauce over the ingredients and cook over moderate heat for 20 to 30 minutes. Yield: 6 servings.

Note: Ingredients for Yosenabe both in kind and amount may be varied according to preference.

Chawanmushi
(Chicken and Shrimp Custard)

- 1 quart chicken broth or Dashi Sauce (see preceding recipe)
- 4 eggs, well beaten
- 1 teaspoon salt
- 1 tablespoon soy sauce
- 1 tablespoon sugar
- 1 cup chopped chicken and shrimp
- ½ cup cooked noodles
- ½ cup cooked green beans, peas or cut asparagus

Combine chicken broth or Dashi with eggs. Put mixture through fine strainer to blend. Add salt, soy sauce, and sugar.

In each of six Japanese bowls with covers or 8 custard cups, place an equal portion of chicken and shrimp, noodles, and green vegetable. Fill bowl or cup with broth mixture. If Japanese bowls are not available, cover custard cup tightly with foil. Set covered bowls or cups in baking pan; fill with hot water nearly to the top of cups and cook in 350°F oven 35 to 40 minutes or until custard does not adhere to blade of knife when inserted. Serve while hot in the cups. Serve in place of soup. Yield: 6 servings.

Note: Mushrooms, bamboo shoots, and water chestnuts may be used. Proportion of egg used is 2 eggs for each pint of mixture.

JORDAN

Mughle (Spicy Rice Dessert)

- 1 cup cream of rice cereal
- 1 tablespoon ground cinnamon
- 1 tablespoon caraway seeds, pulverized
- 2 teaspoons aniseed, pulverized
- 8 cups water
- 2 cups sugar
- 1 cup walnuts, almonds or pine nuts, chopped

Combine rice and spices in a saucepan. Add the water slowly. Bring to boil and cook rapidly for 1 minute, stirring constantly. Add the sugar and boil for 10 minutes or until it is the consistency of custard. Pour into cups; garnish with nuts. Serve hot. Yield: 6 servings.

Kufta Soup (Sour Egg-Drop Meat Ball Soup)

1 pound finely ground mutton
2 tablespoons cream of rice cereal
1 teaspoon salt
½ teaspoon ground cinnamon
½ teaspoon ground allspice
2 tablespoons dried parsley flakes or 1 bunch fresh chopped parsley
3 eggs
6-8 cups chicken broth
4 tablespoons lemon juice

Mix meat, rice, salt, spices and parsley in a large mixing bowl. Add 1 egg and mix thoroughly. Roll mixture into 1-inch balls. Drop balls into boiling chicken broth and simmer for 30 minutes or until balls are cooked. Remove pan from heat. Beat 2 eggs with lemon juice and pour into the hot soup. Lift egg lightly with a fork so that the eggs cook in long strands. Serve immediately. Yield: 6-8 servings.

Tajen (Oven-cooked Vegetables and Meat)

1 pound lean beef, minced
2 small onions, finely chopped
2 teaspoons minced parsley
1 teaspoon salt
¼ teaspoon pepper
2 medium potatoes
2 medium tomatoes
2 small eggplants
2 small squash
1 pound green beans
½ teaspoon salt
¼ teaspoon pepper
2 cups water
2 tablespoons butter

Combine the minced beef, onions, parsley, salt, and pepper. Shape the mixture into small balls, about 1-inch in diameter; set aside. To prepare the vegetables, peel the potatoes, tomatoes, eggplants and squash, and cut into 1-inch cubes; cut the beans in 1-inch lengths. Combine the vegetables with salt and pepper. Pour vegetables into a shallow baking dish; place meat balls on vegetables. Add water and dot with butter. Cook in a 400°F oven for 45 to 60 minutes. Yield: 6 servings.

KENYA

Bean Stew

- 1 cup dried beans
- 4 cups boiling water
- 1 pound beef stew meat, tenderized and cut in 1-inch cubes
- 2 tablespoons oil
- 1 large onion, chopped coarsely
- 2 large potatoes, pared and cubed
- 3 ribs celery, cut in 1-inch slices
- 3 medium carrots, pared and cut in rounds
- 1 cup fresh or frozen corn
- 1 teaspoon curry powder
- 1½ teaspoon salt
- 1 cup boiling water
- ½ pound fresh or frozen Brussels sprouts

Add beans to boiling water in a 3-quart sauce pan or Dutch oven; boil for 2 minutes. Remove from heat and let stand covered for 1 hour. Return to heat and simmer in the same water for 1 hour.

Brown meat in hot oil; add onion and cook until brown. Add meat and onion mixture and all other ingredients, except the Brussels sprouts, to the beans; add 1 cup boiling water. Simmer stew for 1 hour; add sprouts and continue cooking for 15 minutes. Yield: 6 to 8 servings.

KUWAIT

Kharoff

(Stuffed Crown Roast of Lamb)

- 1 pound lean lamb, cut in small cubes
- 1 medium onion, chopped
- 1 cup water
- 1 teaspoon salt
- ¼ teaspoon pepper
- ¼ teaspoon cinnamon
- ¼ teaspoon powdered cardamon
- ¼ teaspoon powdered cloves
- ¼ teaspoon powdered ginger
- 2 cups cooked rice
- ¼ cup raisins
- ¼ cup toasted almonds
- 5-pound crown roast of lamb
- 3 hard-cooked eggs

Simmer minced lamb and onion in water in covered sauce pan for 20 minutes or until liquid is reduced to about ¼ cup. Mix together salt, all of the spices, rice, raisins and half of the almonds. Add meat mixture and toss lightly.

Place lamb roast on rack in a shallow roasting pan; half-fill roast with stuffing. Cut 2 eggs in quarters lengthwise and arrange on top of stuffing. Add remaining stuffing. Cover top of roast and stuffing with aluminum foil. Bake in 325°F oven for 2½ hours or until done. Remove foil during last 15 minutes of roasting. Garnish with remaining egg, sliced, and almonds. Serve with curried rice. Yield: 8 servings.

LAOS

Kengphed (Spiced Fish Chowder)

½ cup pimientos, mashed
1 clove garlic, sliced
½ cup diced onion
2 tablespoons oil
1 pound swordfish steak or other fish steak or fillet, cut in small pieces
1 quart coconut milk (page 27)
2 medium potatoes, sliced and parboiled
1 teaspoon salt
¼ teaspoon pepper

Sauté pimientos, garlic, and onion in hot oil for 5 minutes or until onion is yellow. Add fish and cook over low heat about 5 minutes or until fish is partially cooked. Add coconut milk and potatoes. Simmer for 20 minutes. Add salt and pepper. Serve hot. Yield: 6 servings.

Nham Salad (Fresh Vegetable-Chicken Salad)

1 medium head lettuce
3 tomatoes, peeled and cut into eighths
2 ribs celery, cut in ¼-inch slices
3 scallions, cut in small pieces
2 hard-cooked eggs
1 cup diced cooked chicken
4 tablespoons olive oil
2 tablespoons vinegar
1 tablespoon pickle relish
1 tablespoon monosodium glutamate
½ teaspoon black pepper

Break lettuce in bite-size pieces. Add tomatoes, celery, scallions, chopped whites of eggs, and chicken. Mash egg yolks, add oil, vinegar, pickle relish, monosodium glutamate and pepper. Mix to a smooth paste. Add dressing to salad ingredients and toss lightly until salad is well coated with dressing. Yield: 6 servings.

LEBANON

Sayadiah (Fish and Rice)

- 1 pound fish fillets, cod, halibut or sole
- 4 tablespoons butter
- 1 large onion, chopped
- ½ cup pine nuts
- 1 cup rice
- 1 teaspoon salt
- 2 cups water

Cook fish fillets in 2 tablespoons of butter until light brown. Cook chopped onions and pine nuts in the other 2 tablespoons of butter in second frying pan until onions are yellow but not brown. Grease a 2-quart casserole; place a layer of onions and pine nuts, a layer of fish, and a layer of rice. Repeat layers using all of the ingredients. Add salt to water and pour over all the ingredients. Cover and bake at 350°F for 1 hour or until rice is cooked. Remove cover for last 15 minutes of baking time. Yield: 6 servings.

Pickled Stuffed Peppers

- 6 green peppers
- 2½ cups finely chopped cabbage
- ½ cup chopped carrots
- ½ cup chopped celery
- 1 clove garlic
- 3 tablespoons salt
- 3 cups water, boiled and cooled
- 1⅓ cups vinegar

Wash peppers; cut tops off carefully and remove seeds. Mix cabbage, carrots, and celery, and stuff peppers very tightly with the mixture. Replace tops on stuffed peppers; secure with thread. Place peppers, top side up, in large mouthed glass jar; place garlic in center of jar. Add salt to cooled water; stir to dissolve and add vinegar. Pour this mixture into jar to cover peppers. Seal jar and allow two weeks for peppers to pickle. Serve as a relish. Yield: 6 pickled stuffed peppers.

Tabbouli (Wheat Salad)

½ cup bulgar wheat, finely crushed
Water
1½ cups finely chopped parsley
½ cup finely chopped mint leaves
1 onion, chopped
1 tomato, chopped
¼ cup lemon juice
¼ cup olive oil
½ teaspoon salt
¼ teaspoon pepper

Soak bulgar in water to cover for ½ hour. Drain well; add parsley, mint, onion, and tomato to drained bulgar. Mix lemon juice, oil, salt, and pepper, and add to salad. Toss lightly, coating salad ingredients. Serve on lettuce. Yield: 6 servings.

LIBERIA

Jollof Rice
(Chicken and Meat with Rice)

1 3-pound frying chicken, cut in serving pieces
¼ cup oil
½ pound smoked ham, cubed
2 medium onions, sliced
1 teaspoon salt
¼ teaspoon pepper
½ teaspoon ground allspice
2 1-pound cans tomatoes
1 6-ounce can tomato paste
1 tomato paste can water
¼ pound string beans, fresh or frozen
1 cup raw rice
2 cups water
1 teaspoon salt

Cook chicken in hot oil in Dutch oven or large frying pan until chicken is brown. Add ham, onions, salt, pepper, and allspice; cook until onion is tender, stirring occasionally. Add tomatoes, paste, and water; stir to mix ingredients. Place green beans on top of meat mixture; cover and simmer for 20 minutes or until vegetables are steamed tender.

Cook rice for ten minutes in salted water; drain in a colander. Add rice to meat and vegetables and continue to simmer for 15 minutes or until rice is tender and blended with sauce. Additional water may be added. Yield: 6-8 servings.

Cassava Cake

- 1¼ cups raw grated cassava or minute tapioca
- ½ cup milk
- 1 egg, beaten
- 6 tablespoons butter
- 1 cup sugar
- ¾ cup grated coconut
- ½ cup flour
- 2½ teaspoons baking powder
- Few grains salt
- 1 teaspoon vanilla

Mix cassava or tapioca with milk and egg; let stand for 5 minutes. Cream butter and sugar; add tapioca mixture and coconut to creamed butter and sugar. Mix batter well.

Sift flour, baking powder, and salt; add to batter; stir in vanilla and turn batter into an oiled and floured 8-inch square cake pan. Bake in 400°F oven for about 40 minutes or until done. Cut in squares or rectangles. It is delicious warm with vanilla ice cream Yield: 8 servings.

LIBYA

Couscous (North African Lamb Stew)

- 1½ pounds boneless lean lamb, cut into 2-inch cubes
- ¾ cup olive oil
- 7 large onions, sliced ½-inch thick
- 1 large tomato, cubed
- 1 tablespoon crushed red pepper
- ½ teaspoon allspice
- 2 teaspoons turmeric
- 2 teaspoons salt
- 1 6-ounce can tomato paste
- 1 quart boiling water
- 4 medium potatoes, peeled and quartered
- 1 1-pound can chick-peas or garbanzo
- ½ pound cracked wheat or 1 pound couscous or semolina

Brown the meat in hot oil in deep kettle or Dutch oven with a capacity of at least 3 quarts. Add 3 of the onions, and the tomato. Continue cooking over low heat for 10 minutes. Add the pepper, allspice, turmeric, salt, tomato paste, and water. Cover and simmer for 1 hour; add the remaining onions and potatoes; simmer for 30 minutes, adding water if needed. Add the chick-peas with liquid and simmer for 10 minutes or until mixture is hot.

Cook the cracked wheat or couscous according to package directions. Turn the cooked cracked wheat or couscous into a large serving bowl; pour the meat stew or sauce over the wheat slowly; let the dish stand for 5 minutes before serving to permit wheat to absorb some of the sauce. Yield: 10 servings.

Note: Cracked wheat, bulgar, semolina, or couscous may be used and purchased in special food stores.

Libyan Lamb Soup

- 1½ pounds boneless lean lamb, cut into ½-inch cubes
- 1 medium onion, finely chopped
- ¼ cup olive oil
- 2 tablespoons tomato paste or catsup
- 2 teaspoons salt
- 1 tablespoon crushed red pepper
- 1 quart water
- 1 cup small noodles, uncooked
- 3 tablespoons chopped parsley or fresh mint
- 1½ tablespoons lemon juice

Cook meat and onion in hot oil in deep kettle or Dutch oven for 5 minutes, stirring frequently. Add tomato paste, salt, red pepper, and water. Cover and simmer for 1 hour; add the noodles and additional water, if needed. Cook until noodles are tender; add parsley or mint and lemon juice just before serving. Yield: 6 servings.

LUXEMBOURG

Boeuf à la Mode

- 2 pounds lean beef, cut in 2-inch cubes
- 1 small onion, sliced
- 1 sprig parsley
- 1 pint dry white wine
- ¼ pound beef suet
- 2 teaspoons salt
- ½ cup flour
- ¼ teaspoon pepper
- 1 cup water

Place beef, onion slices, and parsley in a bowl. Add wine; place in refrigerator for 2 days. Turn meat occasionally.

Render suet in large skillet; discard solid pieces. Drain meat; put meat, flour, salt, and pepper in clean paper bag; shake well to coat meat evenly. Brown meat in rendered fat, turning to brown all sides. Add water and the marinating wine to meat; cover and cook over low heat for 2 to 3 hours or until meat is tender. Add more water if necessary to keep sauce thin. Serve with egg noodles and apple sauce flavored with cinnamon. Yield: 6 servings.

Note: During last 30 minutes of cooking period, any combination of the following vegetables may be added: 1½ cups diced carrots, 1½ cups diced turnips, ½ pound small white onions, ½ pound small potatoes.

MADAGASCAR

Varenga (Browned Shredded Beef)

2 pounds boneless chuck, cut in small pieces
Water
2 tablespoons salt
1 clove garlic
1 onion, sliced

Place beef in a 2-quart sauce pan; cover with water; add salt, garlic, and onion. Cover; bring to a boil and simmer for 2 hours or until the meat can be shredded with a fork. Add water, if necessary, during the cooking period.

When the meat is tender, shred mixture and transfer to a 7 x 11 inch baking dish; roast at 400°F. for ½ hour or until meat is browned. Yield: 6 servings.

Soupe à la Malgache (Vegetable Soup)

3 pounds veal bones
2 tablespoons salt
2 quarts water
2 large tomatoes, peeled and diced
1 large onion, peeled and diced
3 medium potatoes, peeled and diced
3 carrots, peeled and diced
1 small turnip, peeled and diced
1 leek (optional)
1 cup string beans (optional)

Place veal bones in a 5-quart sauce pan; add salt and water; bring to a boil and simmer for 1 hour. Add tomatoes and onions and simmer for another 1½ hours. Add remainder of vegetables and simmer until vegetables are tender, about 1 hour.

Remove the veal bones; sieve the vegetables and return to the liquid. Serve thick and hot. Yield: 6 servings.

MALAYSIA

Spicy Lamb Omelet

- 1 pound of lamb, free of bone and fat
- 2 tablespoons vegetable oil
- 1 1½-inch stick cinnamon
- 2 tablespoons onion powder
- ¼ teaspoon nutmeg
- ½ teaspoon white pepper
- 1 teaspoon salt
- 1 cup water
- 6 eggs, slightly beaten

Cut lamb into ½-inch cubes and brown in hot vegetable oil. Drain off fat. Add all ingredients listed except the eggs and simmer until mixture is thick and reduced to about 1½ cups. Let mixture cool. Combine cooled meat mixture and eggs; pour into an oiled shallow baking dish. Cook in a 325°F oven until the eggs are as firm as desired. Yield: 6 servings.

Note: Lamb mixture is very good served over hot buttered noodles.

Daging Goreng (Marinated Beef Strips)

- 2 pounds beef chuck or round steak, tenderized
- 1½ teaspoons turmeric
- 1½ teaspoons pepper
- 1½ teaspoons garlic powder
- 1½ teaspoons onion powder
- 1½ teaspoons salt
- 1½ tablespoons sugar
- 1 cup cooking oil

Slice meat in strips about ¼-inch thick. Combine all seasonings and sprinkle on meat. Let meat stand for 1 hour; turn occasionally to coat all pieces. Heat oil in large frying pan. Put all the meat in hot oil and cook until brown, stirring and turning so that each piece browns. Drain well and serve hot. Yield: 6 servings.

Sambal-Goreng (Shrimp with Green Pepper)

- 1 medium onion, cut fine
- 3 green onions including tops, cut fine
- ¼ cup vegetable oil
- 1 green bell pepper, cut in thin strips
- 3 tomatoes, peeled and cut into cubes
- ½ cup blanched almonds, slivered
- ½ pound fresh shrimp, cleaned and deveined
- ½ teaspoon basil
- ½ teaspoon thyme
- 1 teaspoon salt
- ¼ teaspoon white pepper
- 2 tablespoons flour
- 1 cup coconut milk (page 27) or cream

Sauté onions in oil for about 3 minutes. Add all of the ingredients except the flour and milk or cream; simmer for 3 minutes. Mix flour and ¼ of the milk to a paste; add the remaining milk and then add to mixture. Stir constantly until mixture boils. Serve over rice. Yield: 6 servings.

Inti-puff (Coconut Surprise)

- 6 tablespoons brown sugar
- 6 tablespoons white sugar
- 2 tablespoons cornstarch
- 5 tablespoons water
- 1 4-ounce can shredded coconut
- Plain pastry, using 2 cups flour
- 1 egg, beaten

Combine sugars, cornstarch, and water in saucepan. Bring to a boil while stirring; cook until thickened. Add coconut and stir until blended. Let mixture cool.

Prepare pie dough and roll on floured surface to ⅛-inch thickness. Cut out 4-inch circles, re-rolling dough as necesary. Place 1 teaspoon of coconut mixture on half of each circle. Brush edges with egg; fold circle over and seal edges with fork. Place on cookie sheet; prick tops with fork and brush tops with egg. Bake at 400°F, 20-25 minutes or until golden brown. Cool on wire rack. Yield: 18 Surprises.

MALI

Le To (2-Sauce Stew)

First Sauce:

½ pound ground beef
¼ pound dried fish soaked in 1 cup water or ½ pound fresh fish, flaked
½ teaspoon salt
2 medium onions, diced coarsely
Water
2 teaspoons Filé or 1 tablespoon cornstarch mixed with ¼ cup water

Second Sauce:

½ pound beef, cut in ½-inch cubes
1 tablespoon oil
2 small onions, diced
3 tablespoons tomato purée
½ teaspoon salt
Water

Cornmeal Accompaniment:

1 cup cornmeal
½ teaspoon soda
3½ cups boiling water
½ teaspoon salt

To make First Sauce: combine beef, flaked fish, salt, and onions in a saucepan; cover with water. Cover and bring mixture to a boil; reduce heat and simmer for 20 minutes. If Filé is used, stir into sauce immediately before serving and do not let sauce boil after adding Filé. If cornstarch is used, let sauce simmer for 5 minutes.

To make Second Sauce: brown meat in hot oil in frying pan; add onions and cook for 5 minutes, stirring frequently. Add purée, salt, and water to cover ingredients. Cook covered over low heat for 20 minutes.

To make Cornmeal Accompaniment: stir cornmeal and soda into the boiling water, stirring constantly. Add the salt and cook until mixture is thick. Reduce heat and cook 20 minutes, stirring occasionally.

Combine the two sauces. Serve the cornmeal mixture in a shallow bowl with the 2-Sauces, which is served in a separate dish. Yield: 6 servings.

Note: Filé, a green powder used in Creole cookery, is available in spice sections of food shops. Fresh okra may be used when available to obtain same result as Filé.

MAURITANIA

Michoui (Stuffed Leg of Lamb)

- ⅓ cup raisins
- ⅓ cup pitted dates, chopped
- ⅓ cup dried figs, chopped
- 1½ tablespoons pine nuts
- ¼ cup chopped onion
- ⅔ cup bulgar
- 1½ tablespoons chopped parsley
- 1 teaspoon salt
- ¼ teaspoon ground coriander
- ⅛ teaspoon pepper
- 1 cup stock or bouillon
- 1 5-pound leg of lamb, boned

Combine the first ten ingredients listed with ⅓ cup of the stock or bouillon; mix well. Stuff lamb with this mixture, filling bone cavities well; secure with skewers. Place stuffed leg on a rack in shallow roasting pan and roast in a 325°F oven for 2½ to 3 hours, depending upon how well done meat is preferred. Baste lamb occasionally with the remaining ⅔ cup of broth and meat juices during cooking period. Yield: 6 to 8 servings.

Note: In Mauritania it is the stomach cavity of a whole young sheep that is stuffed.

MEXICO

Capirotada (Bread Pudding)

- 12 slices day-old bread
- ¾ cup cooking fat
- 2½ cups light brown sugar
- 1 teaspoon ground cinnamon
- 1 cup water
- 6 tablespoons butter
- ½ cup cottage cheese
- ½ cup pine nuts

Brush both sides of each slice of bread with melted fat and brown in oven. Make syrup by boiling the sugar, cinnamon and water for 3 minutes. Use 1 tablespoon of butter to grease a 9 x 9 x 2 inch baking pan. Place a layer of bread in the pan; add some cheese, syrup, dots of butter and nuts. Continue layers until all ingredients are used. Place in 350°F oven for 20 minutes or until top layer is brown. Serve hot with fruit or berry sauce. Yield: 6 servings.

Pescado a la Veracruzana (Fish Vera Cruz)

2 pounds red snapper or haddock, cut in serving pieces
2 teaspoons salt
½ teaspoon pepper
Juice of 1 lemon
2 cloves garlic, whole
4 tablespoons oil
3 onions, sliced
1 1-pound can tomatoes
3 tablespoons chopped ripe olives
2 tablespoons capers
6 jalapeño chilis

Rinse fish with cold water; drain and rub with salt, pepper, and lemon juice. Set aside. Cook garlic in the oil to extract flavor. Remove and discard garlic. Cook onions in same oil until yellow. Add the fish, tomatoes, olives, capers, and chilis to the onions and oil. Simmer over low heat until the sauce is thick and the fish is tender. Yield: 6 servings.

Ostiones en Escabeche (Pickled Oysters)

24 oysters in their shells, fresh, frozen, or canned
Cold water
2 teaspoons lemon juice
½ teaspoon salt
½ cup olive oil
2 cloves garlic, mashed
2 peppercorns
4 tablespoons vinegar
8 jalapeño chilis, cut in strips
4 pounds crushed ice, tinted green

Open oysters and place in a sieve over a bowl to catch the natural juices. Pour cold water over oysters, allowing ¼ cup to each pint of oysters. Lift oysters from the water and remove bits of shell. Strain water and reserve for cooking oysters. Place cleaned oysters, ¼ cup of the strained water, lemon juice, and salt in saucepan. Boil for 2 minutes. Drain well. Fry oysters in oil until plump and edges begin to curl. Remove from oil and drain. Add garlic and peppercorns to oil; cook at low heat until garlic is yellow and peppercorns toasted. Remove from fat and add to vinegar. Add oysters, their natural juices and the chilis to the vinegar mixture. Cover and refrigerate for 3 hours. Serve oysters in their shells placed on a tray of ice. Yield: 24 appetizers.

MONGOLIA

Marinated Beef Strips

- 2 pounds top round steak, sliced in strips ¼-inch thick
- ½ cup soy sauce
- 3 tablespoons sugar
- 2 cloves garlic, crushed
- ½ teaspoon pepper
- 2 scallions or green onions, chopped fine

Place strips of beef in mixture of soy sauce, sugar, garlic, pepper, and chopped scallions in a shallow utility dish. Let meat marinate at least 1 hour at room temperature; turn meat occasionally.

Broil each strip for 3 to 5 minutes on each side, depending on how well done meat is preferred. Heat the remaining marinade with meat juices and pour over meat. Serve as entrée or small pieces as appetizers. Yield: 6 servings.

MOROCCO

Tagine (Braised Chicken with Olives)

- 1 3-pound frying chicken, cut into pieces
- 3 tablespoons margarine
- 1 cup water
- 2 medium onions, chopped
- ½ teaspoon ground ginger
- ⅛ teaspoon paprika
- ¼ teaspoon black pepper
- ¼ cup chopped parsley
- 1 7-ounce jar pitted whole green olives
- Water
- 2 tablespoons lemon juice
- 2 tablespoons flour mixed with 2 tablespoons water

Brown chicken in hot margarine in a 3-quart saucepan or in a Dutch oven. Add water, onions, ginger, paprika, black pepper, and parsley to browned chicken. Mix well; cover and simmer for 45 minutes.

Drain olives; cover with cold water in small saucepan and bring to boil for 1 minute. Pour off water; repeat procedure and drain. Add to chicken shortly before serving.

Place chicken with olives on serving dish; pour lemon juice over chicken; thicken remaining liquid with flour and water paste. (Add water, if necessary, to make 1½ cups.) Cook for 3 minutes over low heat, stirring constantly. Pour sauce over chicken and olives. Yield: 6 servings.

Note: Lamb may be used in place of chicken.

Gdra (Chicken with Chick Peas)

- ¾ cup butter
- ⅛ teaspoon saffron
- 1 tablespoon salt
- 1 teaspoon ground pepper
- 6 medium onions, finely chopped
- 2 3-pound stewing chickens, split lengthwise or 4 pounds shoulder of lamb, cut in serving pieces
- 2 1-pound cans chick peas
- Water
- 2 cups rice
- Few sprigs coriander
- 1 large bunch parsley
- Juice of 1 lemon

Melt the butter in a deep kettle or sauce pan; stir in the saffron, salt, pepper and 1 chopped onion. Add chicken or meat and chick peas; cover with water and simmer for 1 hour.

Put rice in clean muslin bag tied securely and place in the kettle containing the meat mixture. Rice should be completely covered with broth. Remove bag of rice after 15 to 20 minutes and keep warm.

Continue cooking until meat is tender. During last hour of cooking, add remainder of onions, coriander and parsley. Serve meat in the center of a large platter with the rice, chick peas, and sauce over the meat. Pour lemon juice over the entire surface. Yield: 8-10 servings.

Kab El Ghzal (Almond Croissants)

- 5½ cups flour
- 6 tablespoons butter
- Water

Almond Filling:

- ½ pound almond paste
- ¼ teaspoon orange extract
- 6 tablespoons butter

Sift flour into a large mixing bowl; make a well in center and pour in 5 tablespoons of melted butter. Blend with a fork; add water slowly and continue blending until mixture is consistency of bread dough and can be kneaded. Knead vigorously on floured board for 20 minutes. Butter board, rolling pin, and tips of fingers lightly, using 1 tablespoon of butter. Divide dough into 4 portions. Roll out on buttered board, then stretch with fingers until dough is ⅛-inch thick. Cut into strips 5-inches wide. Cut the strips crosswise into triangles 3-inches wide at the base.

To make Almond Filling: add orange extract and butter to almond paste and blend thoroughly.

Place 1 teaspoon of Almond Filling on the base and roll up, curving the ends to form a crescent or croissant. Repeat procedure until all of the dough is used. Bake on a cookie sheet in 350°F oven until lightly brown, about 15 minutes. Sizes of croissants may vary according to use and number desired. If pastry shows tendency to puff, prick with pin. Yield: 50 croissants.

NEPAL

Banana Pudding

- 2 cups milk
- 2 tablespoons granulated sugar
- ¼ cup raisins
- 1 tablespoon finely chopped almonds
- 1½ cups diced bananas (3 medium)

Scald milk in a double boiler; add sugar, raisins, nuts, and bananas. Cook for about 10 minutes, stirring constantly until mixture thickens. Remove from heat immediately if small curds show on spoon. Spoon into individual serving dishes, distributing fruit evenly. Cool and refrigerate. Serve cold with a garnish of tart, red jelly. Yield: 6 servings.

Aluko Chop (Potato Cakes)

- ¾ cup finely chopped onions
- 2 tablespoons finely chopped green pepper
- 1 teaspoon salt
- 1½ teaspoons turmeric
- 1 quart freshly mashed potatoes
- 1 cup salad oil
- 2 eggs, slightly beaten

Add onions, green pepper, salt, and turmeric to potatoes and mix thoroughly. Cool mixture until it can be handled easily. Shape into 12 round cakes, using about ⅓ cup of mixture for each cake. Heat oil in a 12-inch frying pan to 380°F or to sizzling point when food is placed in it. Do not let oil smoke. Using a fork, dip each cake into beaten egg and cover completely. Place in hot oil and cook until brown on each side. Cakes will have light, crispy crust. Lift each cake with spatula; drain on absorbent paper. To keep warm until all cakes are fried, place on cooky sheet and in oven at 350°F. Serve hot with entrée. Yield: 6 servings (12 cakes).

Vantako Taruwa (Sautéed Eggplant)

- 1 eggplant, approximately 1½ pounds
- ½ cup flour
- 1 tablespoon salt
- 1½ teaspoons turmeric
- 1 teaspoon freshly ground black pepper
- 1 cup salad oil

Pare the eggplant; cut in ½-inch slices. Coat each slice with mixture of flour, salt, turmeric, and pepper. Heat oil in skillet to 380°F or to point where oil sizzles when eggplant is placed in it. Do not let fat smoke. Place slices of eggplant in fat and brown both sides. Lift slices with spatula; drain on absorbent paper. To keep eggplant warm until all slices are cooked, place on cooky sheet in oven at 350°F. Serve hot with entrée. Yield: 6 servings.

NETHERLANDS

Drie in de Pan (Pancakes)

- 2 cups flour
- 2 teaspoons baking powder
- ½ teaspoon salt
- 1 egg, beaten
- 1 cup milk
- 1 tablespoon melted fat
- ½ cup raisins
- ½ cup currants
- 1 tablespoon grated orange peel

Sift flour, baking powder, and salt into a mixing bowl. Make a well in the center; add egg, milk, and melted fat; beat well. Add raisins, currants, and orange peel. Heat griddle or skillet. Pour batter to form 3 cakes about 3-inches in diameter. Do not crowd. Cook over low heat until rim of each cake is full of bubbles, and underside is golden brown. Loosen with pancake turner and turn. Brown the second side; turn only once. Serve hot with butter and syrup or honey. Yield: 18 cakes.

Gehaktnestjes (Meatloaf Nests)

- ½ pound ground beef
- ½ pound ground veal
- ½ pound ground pork
- ¼ teaspoon pepper
- 1½ teaspoons salt
- ¼ teaspoon nutmeg
- ½ cup chopped onions
- 5 tablespoons butter
- ½ cup soft bread crumbs
- ⅓ cup milk
- 6 hard-cooked eggs
- ½ cup dry bread crumbs
- ½ cup water

Mix ground beef, veal, pork, pepper, salt, and nutmeg. Brown onions in 2 tablespoons butter. Add soft bread crumbs to milk. Combine meat mixture, browned onions and bread crumbs and milk. Divide mixture into six equal portions; flatten each; place a hard-cooked egg in center of each and cover egg with meat, forming a ball. Roll balls in bread crumbs; brown in melted butter (remaining 3 tablespoons) on all sides. Add water and simmer 25 to 30 minutes or until meat is well done. Cut each ball in half; place cut side up. Yield: 6 servings.

NEW ZEALAND

Oyster Stew

1 12-ounce jar fresh oysters and liquid
¼ cup cold water
2 tablespoons butter
2 tablespoons flour
¾ teaspoon salt
Few grains cayenne pepper
4 cups milk
½ cup whipped cream
2 tablespoons minced parsley

Place oysters in a sieve over a bowl to catch the liquid. Pour water over oysters. Lift oysters, one by one; examine for bits of shell. Strain oyster liquid and use for stew.

Melt butter in 2-quart saucepan; stir in flour, salt, and pepper. Gradually add milk and oyster liquid; stir constantly until mixture boils. Add oysters and simmer for 5 minutes, adding more milk, if desired. Serve topped with whipped cream and parsley. Yield: 5 1-cup servings.

NICARAGUA

Old Indians (Tortilla Roll-ups)

½ cup chopped onions
1 large tomato, chopped
2 tablespoons fat
4 cups cooked pork, cut in small pieces
12-18 tortillas, warmed
½ teaspoon salt
¼ teaspoon red pepper
1 6-ounce can of tortilla sauce or tomato sauce
1 egg, well beaten
1 banana, sliced
Grated rind of 1 orange

Cook onions and tomatoes in fat in large frying pan until onions are done. Add meat, 1 tortilla cut in thin strips, salt, pepper, and sauce. Simmer 10 to 15 minutes, stirring frequently. Add egg, banana, and orange peel. Continue simmering for 10 minutes, stirring constantly. Place 1 to 2 tablespoons of mixture on each tortilla and roll, placing edge on underside. Pour remainder of meat mixture over tortilla rolls and serve hot as appetizers. Yield: 12-18 servings.

Ajiaco (Pork and Fruit)

1 pint boiling water
½ pound dried beef
1½ pounds pork chops
2 tablespoons shortening
1 cup onions, chopped
3 tomatoes, chopped
2 chili peppers or ½ teaspoon crushed red peppers
¼ teaspoon red pepper
6 bay leaves
3 tablespoons rice
1½ cups water
3 slices pineapple, cut in chunks
2 ripe bananas, sliced
Sugar or salt to taste

Pour boiling water over dried beef in a 3-quart saucepan; let stand 5 minutes and drain. Cut pork from bones and into small pieces. Pan-fry pork in fat, using 10 to 12-inch frying pan. As pork browns, remove from fat to saucepan with drained dried beef. Add onions, tomatoes, and chili peppers to pan in which pork was browned; simmer for 5 minutes. Add red pepper, bay leaves, and rice. Cook until thick; add water, pineapple, bananas, and meat to the sauce. Cover; simmer gently for 30 minutes or until pork is tender. Stir frequently and add water if needed. Taste, add salt and sugar if desired. Yield: 6 servings.

NIGER

Bondo Gumbo (Lamb Gumbo)

3 pounds lean stewing lamb, cut into 2-inch cubes
2 tablespoons peanut or other vegetable oil
½ cup minced onion
3 tablespoons flour
1 6-ounce can tomato paste
1 4-ounce can pimientoes
1½ teaspoons salt
1 quart water
1 pound fresh okra or 1 10-ounce package frozen

Whole Wheat Balls:

1 cup whole wheat flour
½ cup water
Salted water

Brown lamb in hot oil in large skillet or Dutch oven. Add onion and flour to browned lamb; mix well and let flour brown. Add tomato paste, pimientoes, salt, and water. Simmer for 1½ hours; add okra cut in thin rounds and continue simmering until okra becomes soft. Serve in deep dish with Whole Wheat Balls.

To make Whole Wheat Balls: mix flour and water. Cook, covered in top of double boiler for 30 minutes. Stir; dip out balls of dough and drop into pot of boiling salted water for 10 minutes. Remove with slotted spoon and drain. Yield: 6-8 servings.

NIGERIA

Ewa and Dodo
(Seafood and Black-eyed Peas)

- 2 cups black-eyed peas, dried
- 4 cups boiling water
- ½ cup onion, chopped
- 1 large tomato, chopped
- 1½ to 3 teaspoons crushed red peppers
- 2 tablespoons tomato paste
- 3 tablespoons oil
- 1 7-ounce can tuna or 2 4½-ounce cans shrimp
- 3 large bananas, cut in ¼-inch slices
- ½ teaspoon salt
- 1 cup oil for frying

Wash peas in cold running water; cover with boiling water; boil 2 minutes; remove from heat and soak 1 to 2 hours; simmer in the same water until tender. Add onion, tomato, and dried pepper to peas; cook for 15 minutes. Add tomato paste, oil, and fish to peas; cover and simmer for 10 minutes without stirring. Remove cover; stir and simmer for 5 minutes.

Sprinkle bananas with salt; deep-fat fry in oil until golden brown. Drain on absorbent paper. Serve black-eyed peas (Ewa) with bananas (Dodo). Yield: 6 servings.

Wolof Rice (Steak Stew with Rice)

- 2 pounds sirloin steak or tenderized meat, cut in 12 pieces
- 4½ cups water
- 2 teaspoons salt
- ½ cup peanut oil
- 2 large tomatoes, chopped
- 1 large onion, chopped
- 2 tablespoons tomato paste
- 1½ – 3 teaspoons crushed red peppers
- 1 cup rice

Simmer steak in ½ cup of water to which 1 teaspoon salt has been added, until water is evaporated. Brown steak in ¼ cup hot oil. Set aside and keep warm.

Combine in saucepan, 1 tomato, ½ onion, 1 tablespoon tomato paste, dried red pepper, remaining oil and 2 cups water. Simmer until water is almost evaporated. Add browned meat to tomato mixture and simmer gently until mixture is thick and all water evaporated.

Cook rice in remaining water to which 1 teaspoon of salt has been added, for 15 minutes. Add the remaining onion and tomato, and remaining tomato paste, to the rice. Cover saucepan and simmer for 20 minutes. Combine steak and rice mixtures; simmer uncovered for 10 minutes. If desired, serve steak over rice rather than combining the two mixtures. Yield: 6 servings.

Fish with Coconut and Bulgar

- 3 cups coconut milk (page27)
- 2 tablespoons chopped onion
- 3 medium tomatoes, peeled and quartered
- 1 teaspoon salt
- ½ teaspoon pepper
- 1 pound crayfish, beef, or chicken, cut into bite-size pieces
- 1 cup bulgar

Combine milk, onion, tomatoes, salt, pepper, and fish or meat in a sauce pan; simmer for 5 minutes. Stir bulgar into milk mixture and simmer for 15 minutes or until fish and bulgar are done. Yield: 6 servings.

NORWAY

Fersk Suppe og Kjott
(Beef with Carrots and Cabbage)

- 3 pounds beef bones with marrow
- 3 quarts water
- 3 pounds of beef chuck in 1 piece
- 1 package dried soup mix
- 2 teaspoons salt
- ½ teaspoon pepper
- 6 large carrots, cut in ¼-inch slices
- 1 small head cabbage, cut into eighths
- 2 tablespoons chopped parsley

Sauce:

- 1 cup stock
- 1 small onion, chopped
- 4 teaspoons apple or wine vinegar
- 2 teaspoons sugar
- 1 tablespoon flour, mixed with 3 tablespoons cold water

Boil the bones with 3 quarts of water in a 6-quart Dutch oven or heavy kettle for 1½ hours. Remove the bones. Add meat and dried soup mix to stock; simmer until meat is tender, about 2 hours. Drain stock and chill; remove fat. Return meat to stock; add salt, pepper, carrots and cabbage; cook until vegetables are tender. Remove meat, carrots, and cabbage.

Serve soup garnished with chopped parsley. Slice meat; serve with carrots, cabbage, and sauce.

To make sauce: simmer stock and onion until onion is tender. Add vinegar and sugar; add paste; stir until sauce thickens.

Serve as soup and main dish. Yield: 6-8 servings.

Riskrem (Rice Cream)

- ¾ cup uncooked rice
- 1 cup heavy cream, whipped
- ¼ cup sugar
- ½ teaspoon vanilla
- ¼ cup blanched almonds, slivered

Boil rice according to directions on the package; rinse with cold water and drain well.

Add sugar gradually to cream; fold whipped cream and vanilla into the cold rice. Add the almonds. Pour lightly into serving dish and refrigerate. Serve plain or with fruit or berry sauce. Yield: 6 servings.

PAKISTAN

Baryani Pilau (Pakistani Pilaf)

- 3 large onions, minced
- 2-4 cloves garlic, minced
- 1 tablespoon coriander, ground
- 1 teaspoon black pepper
- 2 teaspoons salt
- 2 pounds lamb, cut into 1¼" cubes
- 4 ounces vegetable shortening
- 6 whole cloves
- 2 cardamom seeds, cracked
- 8 ounces yogurt
- ½ cup water
- 2 pounds uncooked rice
- Salted water
- 1 teaspoon saffron, soaked in 1 tablespoon milk
- ½-1 cup hot water

Mix onion, garlic, coriander, pepper and salt in bowl. Add meat and coat with seasonings; let stand for 1 hour.

Cook cloves and cardamoms in hot oil in a large casserole over low heat for 1 minute. Add meat mixture and sauté until meat loses its pink color. Add yogurt and water to cover meat. Cook over a low-medium flame until meat is almost done, approximately 30 minutes.

Cook rice in salted water until half done; strain; add to meat mixture. Add soaked saffron, and enough water to cook rice. Place a hot, wet cloth over the mixture. Cover the casserole with a tight-fitting lid and place in a 250°F oven for 1½ hours or until rice is done. Occasionally dampen cloth to provide steam for cooking the rice. Yield: 8-10 servings.

Mogul Lamb (Spiced Roast Lamb)

- 1 5-pound leg of lamb, most of fat removed
- 1 cup yogurt
- ½ teaspoon powdered ginger
- ½ teaspoon powdered chili
- 4 cloves garlic, finely minced
- ⅓ cup ground almonds
- ½ teaspoon saffron
- 1 teaspoon salt
- ¼ pound butter

Prick surface of lamb with a fork. Mix together well, all of the ingredients listed except the butter; rub mixture well into the meat. Cover loosely; let seasoned meat stand overnight or for at least 12 hours at room temperature.

Place lamb in a shallow roasting pan; dot surface with butter; roast uncovered in a 350°F oven for 15 minutes. Reduce heat to 300°F and cook for 3 to 4 hours. Baste frequently with meat juice from roaster. Place roast on hot serving platter. Remove excess fat from juices; heat and serve with roast. Yield: 8 to 10 servings.

PANAMA

Carimanolas (Panama Fritters)

- ½ pound pork
- 1 small tomato
- 1 small onion
- 1 tablespoon oil
- ¼ teaspoon oregano
- ½ teaspoon salt
- ¼ teaspoon black pepper
- ½ teaspoon crushed red peppers
- 2 teaspoons chopped parsley
- 1 hard-cooked egg, chopped
- 2 pounds sweet potatoes, steamed and mashed
- 1 egg, beaten
- Fat for frying

Grind pork, tomato, and onion in a food chopper, using medium blade. Cook this mixture in oil in heavy frying pan about 15 minutes or until pork loses its pink color. Add the seasonings, parsley, and the chopped egg; stir gently to mix well.

Add the beaten egg to potatoes and knead to make a dough.

On floured board, pat or roll flat about 3 tablespoons of potato dough. Fill the dough with 1 teaspoon of the meat mixture, bringing the dough up, over, and around the meat, similar to the shape of football. Repeat until all of dough and filling are used. Fry the balls in deep fat at 375°F for 4 to 5 minutes or until golden brown. Serve hot. Yield: 6 servings or 18 to 20 fritters.

Note: Original recipe calls for yuca which is not readily available. Dry, starchy type of sweet potato is excellent substitute.

PARAGUAY

Kiveve (Squash Cream)

1 pound butternut squash or other winter squash
Boiling water
¼ teaspoon salt
2 tablespoons margarine or butter
¾ cup cornmeal
2 tablespoons sugar
¼ pound mild Cheddar cheese, diced

Peel squash and cut into small pieces; place in 1½ quart saucepan; cover with boiling, salted water. Cover; cook until tender; drain and mash the squash. Stir in the fat, cornmeal, and sugar. Cook in top of double boiler over direct heat for 5 minutes, stirring constantly. Cover and place on double boiler which is ⅓ full of boiling water. Cook over low heat for 30 minutes. Add the cheese to the cooked mixture; blend and serve either hot or cold, with milk, or as a side dish with broiled fish. Yield: 6 servings.

Chipa Paraguay (Bread)

6 tablespoons margarine
1 teaspoon anise seed
3 eggs
1 cup Parmesan or Cheddar cheese, grated
6 tablespoons milk
2½ cups potato flour
½ teaspoon salt

Cream margarine and anise seeds. Add the eggs, one at a time, and beat well. Fold in grated cheese; add alternately, milk and sifted flour and salt. Mix until dough is smooth. Shape dough into a long roll; cut into 12 equal portions. Roll each portion with hand to form a smaller roll, and place on greased baking sheet in shape of doughnut. Bake in 375°F oven about 35 minutes or until lightly browned. Yield: 6 servings.

Note: 2 teaspoons of baking powder may be added to make a lighter bread.

Polenta Dulce (Cornmeal Cream)

3 cups milk
¾ cup cornmeal
¾ cup sugar
⅛ teaspoon salt
Flavoring, choice of:
¼ teaspoon anise seed or
½ teaspoon cinnamon or
¾ teaspoon vanilla

Combine milk, cornmeal, sugar, and salt in 1½-quart saucepan. Add anise seed or the cinnamon. Cook over a very low heat for 20 minutes, stirring constantly, until mixture thickens, or in double boiler as in Kiveve (see previous page). When done, add vanilla, if vanilla is choice of flavoring. Serve very cold with or without milk. Yield: 6 servings.

PERU

Arroz Jimeno (Veal and Pork with Rice)

12 thin slices of veal steak (about 1½ pounds)
6 thin slices of pork steak
1 teaspoon salt
½ teaspoon pepper
¼ cup flour
6 tablespoons oil
½ cup sherry
1 cup water
1 tablespoon cornstarch with 4 tablespoons water
1 medium onion, diced
1 medium green pepper, diced
1 medium red pepper, diced
1 clove garlic, crushed
2 tablespoons butter
2½ cups cooked rice
2 tablespoons raisins
2 tablespoons sliced almonds
2 hard-cooked eggs, chopped
½ cup cooked peas
2 tablespoons minced parsley

Season veal and pork with salt and pepper; dust lightly with flour. Cook in separate pans.

Brown veal quickly in ⅔ of hot oil. When brown, add sherry; simmer for 5 minutes; remove veal. Add half of water to wine sauce; thicken with cornstarch paste. Simmer for 5 minutes. Return veal to sauce and keep warm.

Brown pork in remaining oil; add remaining water and simmer until water evaporates and pork is tender and well cooked. Add more water if necessary; pork should be brown for serving.

Cook onion, peppers, and garlic in butter slowly until tender, but not browned. Add rice, raisins, almonds and eggs. Cover and place in 300°F oven, or over hot water, to keep warm.

Place rice mixture in a mound in center of serving platter; place meat around rice; pour sauce over meat. Garnish rice with green peas and the meat with chopped parsley. Yield: 6 servings.

Leche Asada (Custard with Cognac)

1 14½-ounce can evaporated milk
⅓ cup water
4 tablespoons cognac
4 to 6 tablespoons sugar
3 eggs, slightly beaten
⅛ teaspoon cinnamon
⅛ teaspoon nutmeg

Add water to evaporated milk; scald milk. Combine other ingredients; stir in the hot milk; pour into individual molds of oven glassware or earthenware. Set the molds in a baking pan; pour in hot water nearly to the top of the molds. Bake at 350°F for 45 minutes or until inserted knife comes out clean. Serve cold as dessert, plain or with cream or fruit sauce. Yield: 6 servings.

PHILIPPINES

Pancit Guisado (Meat and Seafood with Noodles)

1 4½-ounce can shrimp
¾ cup cooked pork cubes
¾ cup cooked ham cubes
1 5-ounce canned chicken
4 cloves garlic
1 medium onion, sliced
2 tablespoons fat
3 tablespoons soy sauce
1 teaspoon salt
½ teaspoon pepper
1½ cups chicken stock
1 cup coarsely shredded cabbage
6-ounce package home-style noodles
1 lemon, sliced

Cook shrimp, pork, ham, chicken, garlic, and onion in fat until onions are yellow. Remove a small portion of each for garnishing and set aside. To the remaining mixture add the soy sauce, salt, pepper, ½ cup chicken stock, and cabbage. Stir; cover and simmer about 10 minutes, or until cabbage is cooked but still crisp.

Boil the noodles according to directions on package until almost done. Drain and add to meat and cabbage mixture. Add remainder of chicken stock; cover and simmer for 15 minutes. Serve in deep platter; garnish with food held for this purpose and with thin slices of lemon. Serve with soy sauce, if desired. Yield: 6 servings.

Note: Amounts and kinds of meat can be varied according to available left-overs and tastes.

Asado de Carajay (Pork Paprika)

- 1½ pounds boneless pork shoulder butt, sliced in long slices
- ¼ teaspoon freshly ground pepper
- 1½ teaspoon salt
- 1 clove garlic, crushed
- 3 tablespoons oil
- 1 bay leaf
- ¼ cup vinegar
- 1 tablespoon paprika
- 1 cup water
- 4 medium onions, quartered
- 1 medium tomato, sliced

Brown pork with pepper, salt, and garlic in oil. Add bay leaf, vinegar, and paprika. Continue browning for about 10 minutes; add water, onions, and tomato. Cover; simmer mixture for 1 hour or until pork is done. Check occasionally and add water if necessary. Yield: 4-6 servings.

POLAND

Suflet Owocowy (Fruit Soufflé)

- 2 teaspoons melted butter
- 2 tablespoons granulated sugar
- 1 cup fruit jam
- 2 tablespoons lemon juice
- 1 teaspoon grated lemon rind
- 3 egg whites, beaten stiff

Brush 6 custard cups with melted butter and coat thoroughly with sugar.

Mix jam and lemon juice. Place over low heat, stir constantly, and bring to boiling point. Remove from heat and add lemon rind.

Fold 1 tablespoon of jam at a time into egg whites. When all of jam is added, beat until mixture holds its shape. Spoon mixture into baking dishes. Fill completely and swirl the tops. Place dishes on baking sheet and bake in a 325°F oven 30 minutes or until top is lightly browned and firm to touch. Serve immediately with a dessert sauce. Yield: 6 servings.

Bigos (Hunter's Stew)

- 1 cup chopped onion
- 2 tablespoons butter
- 1 small head white cabbage, shredded finely
- 1 quart sauerkraut
- 6 large whole mushrooms, sliced
- 4 cups diced Polish sausage and any combination of roasted beef, veal, pork or lamb
- 2 bouillon cubes dissolved in 1 cup water or gravy from roast
- 2 sour apples, peeled and diced
- 1 tablespoon plum marmalade or 4 pitted prunes
- 1 cup tomato purée
- 1 bay leaf
- 1 teaspoon salt
- ½ teaspoon freshly ground pepper
- ¾ cup red wine
- 1 clove garlic, crushed

Cook onion in butter until golden brown. Use a 3-quart casserole or baking dish; add all of the ingredients as listed, except the wine and garlic to the casserole. Place covered casserole in a 300°F oven and cook for 2 hours. Add the wine and garlic and continue cooking for 20 minutes. Yield: 8 servings.

Note: Bigos should be prepared at least 3 days in advance of serving, and reheated once or twice a day during the marination. Refrigerate in a glass or non-metal container.

Chlodnik (Cold Vegetable and Yogurt Soup)

- 1 1-pound can of beets
- 1 fresh cucumber, diced
- 1 pickle, diced
- ½ cup diced radishes
- 1 clove garlic, crushed with ½ teaspoon salt
- 1 quart yogurt
- 1 bouillon cube dissolved in beet liquid
- 12 shrimp, cooked and deveined, or ½ pound roast veal, cubed
- 2 hard-cooked eggs, sliced
- ½ teaspoon sugar, optional
- 1 tablespoon chopped onion
- 2 tablespoons chopped parsley
- 2 tablespoons chopped dill

Drain canned beets and cut in fine strips; save beet liquid. Add beets, cucumber, pickle, radishes and garlic to yogurt in a 2-quart bowl. Stir the beet juice and bouillon into the yogurt mixture; add the shrimp or veal, hard-cooked eggs, sugar, and onion. Serve cold with parsley and dill sprinkled on top. Yield: 6 servings.

Note: This soup is usually served in Poland during the harvest season.

Grzyby w Smietanie
(Mushrooms with Sour Cream)

- 1 medium onion, sliced
- 3/4 pound mushrooms, sliced
- 4 tablespoons margarine
- 1 tablespoon flour
- 2 tablespoons milk
- 1 cup sour cream
- 1/2 teaspoon salt
- 1/8 teaspoon pepper
- 1/8 teaspoon paprika

Brown onions and mushrooms lightly in hot fat in frying pan. Sprinkle with flour; blend and brown slightly. Add milk and 1/2 cup sour cream; continue cooking over low heat until onions and mushrooms are tender. Add seasonings and remainder of sour cream. Heat and serve as an appetizer on small toast rounds. Yield: 24 to 30 appetizers.

PORTUGAL

Bachalhau do Céu (Heavenly Codfish)

- 2 pounds potatoes, uniform size, boiled in jackets
- 2 tablespoons butter
- 1/4 cup milk
- 2 onions, sliced
- 1/4 cup olive oil
- 2 pounds fresh or frozen codfish
- 8 hard-cooked eggs, sliced
- Béchamel sauce
- 1 egg yolk

Béchamel Sauce:

- 1/4 cup butter
- 1/4 cup flour
- 1/2 teaspoon salt
- 1/8 teaspoon pepper
- 1 1/2 cups hot chicken stock
- 1 cup scalded milk
- 2 tablespoons tomato paste or 1 egg yolk

Drain; cool and peel boiled potatoes. Slice about 3/4 of the potatoes; mash remaining 1/4 and season with butter and milk.

Cook onions in hot oil in 12-inch skillet until onions are yellow; add codfish, cut in small pieces. Cook for 30 minutes over low heat.

To make Béchamel Sauce: melt butter; add flour, salt, and pepper; gradually add chicken stock and milk. Cook over low heat 3 to 5 minutes. Add tomato paste to give flavor and color or add 1 slightly beaten egg yolk for yellow sauce.

Grease a 2-quart casserole. Place a layer of codfish in the casserole, then a layer of sliced potatoes, eggs and Béchamel sauce. Continue layers in order given using all ingredients; top with mashed potatoes. Brush with beaten egg yolk. Bake in 350°F oven for 45 minutes or until potatoes are golden brown. Yield: 6-8 servings.

Carne Assada à Portuguesa
(Portuguese Pot Roast)

- 4 to 5 pounds boned rump roast
- 2 cups red wine
- 3 large onions, sliced
- 1 clove garlic
- 2 teaspoons salt
- ¼ teaspoon pepper
- ¼ cup fat
- 2 large tomatoes, thickly sliced

Marinate the roast for at least 24 hours in sauce of red wine, 2 of the onions, garlic, salt, and pepper (in refrigerator). Turn meat occasionally. Cook remaining sliced onion in hot fat in Dutch oven or heavy kettle with lid, until onion is brown; remove onion and save. Brown drained and dried roast on all sides in hot fat; add browned onion and marinade to roast; add water to cover approximately ⅔ of the meat. Cover tightly; simmer, turning meat occasionally, for 4 to 4½ hours or until meat is fork tender. During last hour of cooking, add sliced tomatoes; remove cover during last 30 minutes. Sauce can be strained and thickened, if desired. Yield 8-10 servings.

ROMANIA

Pickled Egg Plant

- 1 medium egg plant
- 1 teaspoon salt
- ½ cup flour
- ½ cup oil
- 3 tablespoons water
- 3 tablespoons vinegar
- 1 bay leaf
- 1 clove garlic, minced
- ½ teaspoon powdered ginger

Cut eggplant in ½-inch slices, leaving skin on; salt and let stand ½ hour. Dry with paper towels. Dip slices in flour and sauté in hot oil until slightly browned and tender. Drain on paper towels.

Combine water, vinegar, bay leaf, garlic, and ginger. Heat for 5 minutes and pour sauce over egg plant. Refrigerate and serve very cold. Yield: 6-8 servings.

RWANDA

Beef Stew à la Rwanda

1½ pounds beef stew meat, cut in 1-inch cubes
1 medium onion, diced
2 tablespoons oil
4 green bananas, available in Spanish food shops
4 tablespoons lemon juice
4 tablespoons tomato sauce
1 teaspoon salt
½ teaspoon ground sage
¼ teaspoon pepper
Water

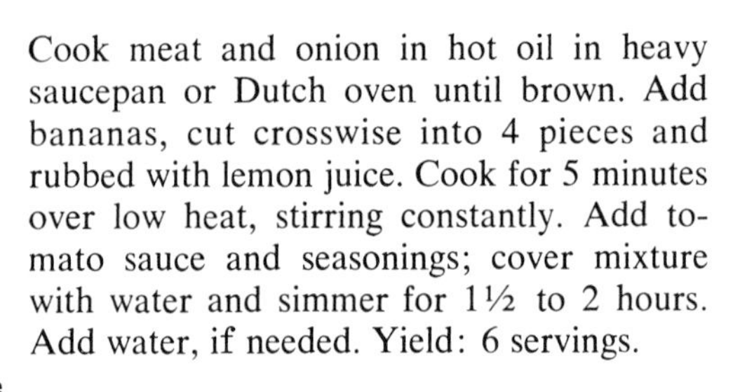

Cook meat and onion in hot oil in heavy saucepan or Dutch oven until brown. Add bananas, cut crosswise into 4 pieces and rubbed with lemon juice. Cook for 5 minutes over low heat, stirring constantly. Add tomato sauce and seasonings; cover mixture with water and simmer for 1½ to 2 hours. Add water, if needed. Yield: 6 servings.

SAUDI ARABIA

Tadjin Ahmar
(Lamb with Saffron)

3 pounds lean lamb, cut into 2-inch strips
3 tablespoons butter
1 large onion, finely chopped
2 tablespoons flour
Water
¼ to ½ teaspoon saffron
1 small stick cinnamon
1 tablespoon salt
⅛ teaspoon pepper
1 cup large dried prunes
1 tablespoon grated orange peel
1 tablespoon sugar

Brown the lamb in the butter; remove the meat and add onion to remaining fat and cook until brown. Add the flour to the onion and continue cooking until mixture is deep brown, stirring continuously.

Add onion and flour mixture to the meat in a 2-quart casserole; cover with hot water; stir in saffron, cinnamon, salt, and pepper. Cook in a 325°F oven for about 2 hours or until meat is almost tender. Add the prunes, which have been soaked in cold water for 1 to 2 hours. Continue cooking meat for another hour; stir in orange peel and sugar. Serve immediately. Yield: 8 to 10 servings.

Fouja Djedad (Chicken Stuffed Apples)

6 baking or cooking apples
1 cup chicken, chopped
¼ teaspoon ground cloves
6 teaspoons sugar
½ cup buttered bread crumbs

Wash and core the apples, making cavity for the filling. Combine chicken with the ground cloves; fill the apple cavities with the meat. Place stuffed apples in shallow baking dish. Sprinkle each apple with 1 teaspoon sugar; top with bread crumbs. Cover and bake at 375°F for 45 minutes or until apples are tender. Remove cover and cook for 5 minutes to brown bread crumbs. Yield: 6 servings.

Munkaczina (Zesty Orange Salad)

3 large oranges
2 sweet onions
3 tablespoons oil
3 tablespoons salad vinegar
⅛ teaspoon cayenne pepper
½ teaspoon salt
12 pitted ripe olives, sliced

Peel oranges and onions; slice thinly. Arrange the slices alternately in a serving bowl; pour over slices dressing of oil, vinegar, pepper, and salt. Let salad marinate for 1 hour at room temperature before serving. Top with slices of ripe olives. Yield: 6 servings.

SENEGAL

Beignets (Fritters)

1½ cups sifted flour
1½ teaspoons baking powder
¼ teaspoon salt
1 egg, well beaten
⅔ cup milk
1 teaspoon vanilla
2 drops orange extract

Sift dry ingredients together; stir in beaten egg mixed with milk, vanilla and orange extract. Stir until smooth; drop from a spoon into deep-fat heated to 375°F and fry a deep golden brown.

For fruit fritters, use 6 bananas, cut in thick slices, or sections of 3 oranges with seeds and pith removed. Add fruit to batter just before frying. Yield: 6 servings.

Boulettes (Fish Balls in Sauce)

- 3 cloves garlic
- ½ cup chopped parsley
- 2 large tomatoes
- 3-inch slice French bread, about 2 cups
- 2 pounds cod or haddock fillets
- 1 onion
- 2 teaspoons salt
- ¼ teaspoon pepper
- Oil for frying

Sauce:

- 1 onion, chopped
- 3 tablespoons tomato paste
- 2 cups water
- 1 teaspoon salt
- Few grains cayenne pepper
- 2 tablespoons vinegar

Put first 6 ingredients through food chopper, using fine blade. Add salt and pepper. Blend mixture well; form into balls about 1½-inches in diameter. Fry in 1-inch of oil heated to 375°F until well browned.

To make sauce: fry onion in 2 tablespoons oil left from frying balls; add tomato paste, ¼ cup water, and seasonings; mix well. Add remaining water and cook until thick; stir in vinegar and fish balls; simmer for 1 hour. Serve as appetizers. Yield: 6-8 servings.

SIERRA LEONE

Banana Fritters

- 6 bananas, well ripened
- 1 cup rice or wheat flour
- ¼ cup sugar dissolved in ¼ cup water
- ½ to 1 teaspoon nutmeg
- Fat for frying

Mash bananas with a fork or use blender to make pulp; add the flour, sugar dissolved in water, and nutmeg. Add water, if needed, to make batter of pancake consistency. Mix well and fry like pancakes in oiled frying pan until golden brown. Yield: 24 small pancakes.

SOMALIA

Huris Hilib (Veal with Tomato Topping)

½ green pepper, sliced
2 small potatoes, pared and quartered
Water
½ cup chopped onion
1 pound veal, cut in ½-inch cubes
2 tablespoons oil
1 teaspoon salt
¼ teaspoon white pepper
1 teaspoon basil
½ teaspoon crushed garlic
1 fresh tomato, peeled and sliced

Boil pepper and potatoes in a saucepan with water to cover until vegetables are half cooked. Grind in a food chopper, using fine blade. Cook the onion and the meat in the oil for 15 minutes or until brown; add the potato mixture and the seasonings to the meat. Put into greased casserole; place slices of tomato on top of mixture. Cover and cook in a 325°F oven for 20 minutes. Yield: 6 servings.

SOUTH AFRICA

Yellow Peach Pickle

1 29-ounce can sliced yellow peaches
⅔ cup peach juice
1 cup vinegar
1 teaspoon peppercorns
1 teaspoon coriander seeds
1 teaspoon whole allspice
½ teaspoon salt
⅓ cup brown sugar
½ teaspoon turmeric
1 teaspoon curry powder
1 teaspoon cornstarch
½ cup chopped onion
1 hot chili pepper, chopped or ½ teaspoon crushed red peppers

Drain peaches and measure peach juice. Simmer peach juice and vinegar with peppercorns, coriander seeds, and whole allspice, tied loosely in a muslin bag for 10 minutes.

Mix salt, sugar, turmeric, curry powder, and cornstarch; add ½ cup of pickle mixture; blend and add to pickle mixture. Cook until thickened, stirring constantly. Add onion, peaches, and chili pepper; cook for 10 minutes. Remove spice bag; fill pint jars and seal, if not to be used soon. Serve as a relish with chicken, turkey, lamb, or fish. Yield: 2 pints.

Sosaties (Skewered Lamb with Sauce)

1 leg of lamb
1 teaspoon salt
½ teaspoon pepper
1 cup vinegar
1 medium onion, thinly sliced
12 dried apricot halves, cut in small pieces
½ teaspoon curry powder
2 tablespoons sugar
2 cups water
½ pound fat salt pork, cut in 1-inch squares and ½-inch thick
2 tablespoons cornstarch
½ cup cold water

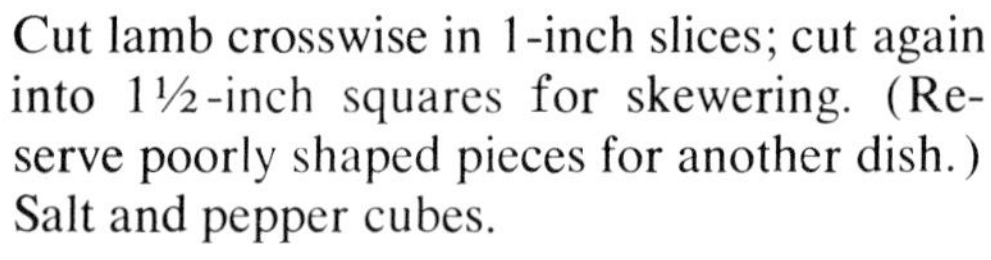

Cut lamb crosswise in 1-inch slices; cut again into 1½-inch squares for skewering. (Reserve poorly shaped pieces for another dish.) Salt and pepper cubes.

Prepare a marinating sauce of vinegar, onion, apricots, curry powder, sugar, and water. Boil for 3 minutes; cool and pour over lamb in a deep container. Add water, if needed for sauce to cover lamb. Refrigerate lamb with sauce for 2 days.

Remove lamb and drain. Use 12 skewers and alternate lamb and fat salt pork. Grill over red-hot coals or broil under direct oven heat until meat is brown and tender.

Heat marinating sauce to which paste of cornstarch and water has been added. Cook until sauce thickens; serve the "Sosaties" with its sauce, and chutney or Yellow Peach Pickle. Yield: 12 Sosaties.

SPAIN

Carbonda (Sweet and Sour Beef with Fruit)

¼ cup butter
4 medium onions, sliced
1 large tomato, peeled and sliced
1½ pounds ground beef
1 teaspoon salt
¼ teaspoon black pepper
1 cup beef stock
2 pears, peeled and sliced
2 peaches, peeled and sliced
4 plums, sliced
4 medium potatoes, diced
¼ cup seedless raisins

Sauté the onion in butter until lightly browned. Add the tomato and cook for 2 minutes. Add the ground beef, stir well and cook for 2 minutes. Add salt, pepper, beef stock. Cover and simmer slowly for 1 hour. Add the fruit and potatoes; cook until potatoes are tender. Do not overcook. Add raisins. Stir. Allow to stand for 1 minute. Serve hot. Yield: 6 servings.

Zarzuela de Pescado a la Levantina
(Levantine Seafood Bake)

- 12 shrimp, shelled and deveined
- 1/4 cup flour mixed with 1/4 teaspoon salt
- 1/2 cup oil for frying
- 1/2 pound mullets
- 1/2 pound squid
- 1/2 pound hake
- 1/2 pound eel
- 1 large onion, chopped
- 3 cloves garlic, chopped
- 1/2 teaspoon paprika
- 1/4 teaspoon saffron
- 3 tablespoons tomato paste
- 1/2 teaspoon salt
- 1/8 teaspoon black pepper
- 12 clams
- Parsley
- Lemon wedges

Coat shrimp with seasoned flour; fry in hot oil until brown. Remove shrimp from oil and drain; place shrimp in a casserole. Clean and cut into cubes all of the fish, except the clams; place fish cubes over the shrimp.

Cook onion in remaining oil until brown; add garlic, paprika, saffron, tomato paste, salt, and pepper; simmer for 5 minutes. Pour this sauce over the fish in the casserole.

Clean and dry clams; steam in 1/2 cup water in covered frying pan until shell opens. Remove top shell and then place clams around the edge of the casserole; pour remaining liquid from clams over the fish. Cook for 15 minutes in a 400°F oven. Garnish with chopped parsley and lemon wedges. Yield: 6 servings.

Pollo a la Pepitoria
(Chicken with Sherry and Almonds)

- 1 3-pound frying chicken, cut for frying
- 1/2 cup flour
- 1 teaspoon salt
- 1/4 teaspoon pepper
- 1 egg, beaten
- 1 cup dry bread crumbs
- 1 cup oil for frying
- 1/2 cup chopped onion
- 1 cup cooking sherry
- 3 cups chicken broth
- 1/2 teaspoon saffron
- 1 tablespoon chopped parsley
- 1 bay leaf
- 1 clove garlic, chopped
- 12 dry almonds, chopped finely
- 2 hard-cooked egg yolks
- 2 tablespoons flour mixed with 4 tablespoons broth

Coat chicken with flour seasoned with salt and pepper; dip each piece in beaten egg and then into bread crumbs. Place breaded chicken in hot fat in large frying pan and cook until brown. Remove chicken from fat, fry onion in remaining fat until brown; drain off excess oil. Return chicken to pan with onions; add sherry and heat slowly; add broth to cover chicken. Add saffron, chopped parsley and bay leaf; cover tightly and cook over low heat or in a 325°F oven for 30 to 40 minutes or until chicken is tender. Stir during cooking.

Brown garlic in oil; make a paste of garlic, almonds, and egg yolk; add flour and broth mixture to paste; mix well.

Remove chicken from pan when tender and stir paste into remaining broth slowly, stirring constantly. Bring to boiling point; reduce heat and simmer for 5 minutes. Return chicken to sauce; simmer until well heated. Yield: 6 servings.

SUDAN

Shorba (Peanut Butter Soup)

2 pounds beef bones
½ pound ground lean beef
3 pints water
1 onion
2 cloves garlic
6 peppercorns
1½ teaspoons salt
½ stick cinnamon
2 cardamon seeds
2 tablespoons peanut butter
Juice of ½ lemon

Bring bones, ground meat, and water to a boil; add onion, garlic, peppercorns and salt. Boil for ½ hour; add cinnamon and cardamon seeds and continue boiling for 1 hour; drain. Combine peanut butter and ¼ cup of the stock, and add to remaining drained stock; simmer for 3 minutes; add lemon juice. Yield: 6 servings.

Shorbat Robe (Yogurt and Cucumber Salad)

2 cucumbers
1 pint yogurt
½ teaspoon salt
⅛ teaspoon garlic powder
⅛ teaspoon black pepper

Peel and chop cucumbers; combine with yogurt, salt, garlic powder, and pepper. Serve on lettuce. Yield: 6 servings.

SWEDEN

Jansson's Frestelse
(Potatoes and Anchovies au Gratin)

- 2 onions, thinly sliced
- 3 tablespoons butter or margarine
- 5 medium potatoes, peeled
- 20 Swedish anchovy fillets
- 1½ cups light cream

Cook onions in 1 tablespoon of fat until yellow. Cut potatoes into lengthwise strips about ¼-inch thick. Butter a 2-quart casserole or baking dish; place layers of potatoes, anchovies, and onions in the casserole, ending with a layer of potatoes. Pour a small amount of the juice from anchovies over the top to add flavor to the dish. Dot the top with remaining butter. Pour cream over top; bake in 350°F oven for 1 hour or until potatoes are done. Serve hot. Yield: 6 servings.

Almond-Apple Pie

- 1½ cups sugar
- 1 cup butter
- 1 cup flour
- 1 cup almonds, finely ground
- 6 large green apples, pared, cored, and sliced thin
- ½ cup whipping cream

Cream 1 cup of sugar and butter; add flour and almonds to creamed mixture and blend until dough is smooth.

Butter a 9-inch pie pan; cover with half of the dough; fill with apple slices. Sprinkle remaining ½ cup of sugar over apples. Cover with remaining dough and bake in a 350°F oven for 45 minutes. Serve lukewarm with chilled whipped cream. Yield: 6 servings.

SYRIAN ARAB REPUBLIC

Menazzeleh (Unusual Meat Pie)

- 1 pound chopped beef
- 1 large onion, chopped
- 1 clove garlic, minced
- 2 tablespoons oil
- ½ teaspoon salt
- 1 teaspoon pepper
- 2 tomatoes, peeled and chopped or ¾ cup stewed tomatoes
- ⅓ cup finely cut parsley
- ½ to 1 teaspoon cumin
- 2 tablespoons chopped mint or dill
- 4 eggs, beaten

Brown the chopped beef, onion, and garlic in hot fat in medium or large frying pan. Add salt, pepper, tomatoes, parsley, cumin, and fresh mint or dill. Cook over low heat until the mixture is well blended. Stir eggs into the meat mixture; cook over low heat until eggs are set. Serve in pie-shaped wedges. Yield: 6 servings.

Sheik el Mah'shi (Stuffed Zucchini)

- 8 zucchini squash, uniform size
- 1 pound ground beef or lamb
- 1 medium onion, finely chopped
- 4 tablespoons margarine
- ½ cup pine nuts
- 1 teaspoon salt
- ⅛ teaspoon pepper
- ½ cup water

Yogurt Sauce:

- 2 cups yogurt
- 2 teaspoons cornstarch
- ¼ teaspoon salt
- Few grains pepper

Wash squash and cut off ends; core squash, being careful to have squash whole and peel unbroken.

Brown the meat and onions in 1 tablespoon of margarine. In a small pan, brown pine nuts in 1 tablespoon of margarine. Combine meat and nuts; add salt and pepper. Cool mixture slightly and stuff the cored zucchini squash with the meat mixture.

Fry the stuffed squash in the remaining margarine until all sides are browned. Add water; cover and simmer until squash are tender. Serve with Yogurt Sauce.

To make Yogurt Sauce: combine yogurt and cornstarch; heat to boiling point, but do not boil; add salt and pepper.

Yield: 6 servings.

Ma'alubi (Veal with Rice and Eggplant)

- 1½ pounds veal
- 3 large onions, cut in quarters
- 2 tablespoons oil
- 1½ teaspoons salt
- ½ teaspoon pepper
- 1 cup water
- 1 medium eggplant
- ⅓ cup oil for frying
- 2 cups rice
- 1 cup tomato sauce
- 3 cups water
- 2 teaspoons salt
- 2 tablespoons almonds, sliced
- 2 tablespoons pine nuts

Brown veal and onions in hot oil in Dutch oven or heavy sauce pan. Add salt, pepper, and water; simmer gently until meat is tender.

Peel eggplant and slice into ¼-inch slices; let stand for 20 minutes and then fry in hot oil. Remove eggplant as it browns and keep warm. Fry rice in remaining fat until yellow; add tomato sauce, water, and salt to rice. Cover and simmer until liquid has been absorbed.

When meat is tender, place fried eggplant slices carefully over meat until meat surface is completely covered. Simmer this mixture for about 10 minutes without stirring. Place cooked rice on top of eggplant; smooth top surface of rice. Place a large serving plate over the top of the pan; turn pan upside down on plate. Sprinkle almonds and pine nuts on top of meat and serve hot with Yogurt and Cucumber Salad (page 110). Yield: 8 to 10 servings.

THAILAND

Tom Yum Gai (Hot and Sour Chicken Soup)

- 6 cups chicken broth
- 2 teaspoons lemon juice
- ¼ teaspoon crushed red peppers
- 1 tablespoon soy sauce
- 1 large chicken breast, cooked and cut into shreds

Bring broth to a boil; add lemon juice, pepper and soy sauce. Add salt, if needed. Add shredded chicken breast; simmer for 3 minutes. Serve with fried noodles. Yield: 6 servings.

Note: Bouillon cubes are not satisfactory for this soup.

Spicy Roast Pork with Pineapple

- 3 to 4 pounds pork loin roast
- 2 teaspoons ground coriander
- 1 clove garlic, crushed
- ½ teaspoon salt
- 1 teaspoon pepper
- 3 tablespoons soy sauce
- 1 tablespoon wine vinegar
- 1 tablespoon sugar
- 1 20-ounce can sliced pineapple

Have backbone separated from meat to make carving easier. Combine coriander, garlic, salt, and pepper; rub this mixture into the roast on all surfaces. Place roast in a shallow roasting pan; cover loosely with foil and roast in a 300°F oven for 2½ hours. Remove foil; baste with mixture of soy sauce, vinegar, and sugar several times; continue cooking uncovered for 30 minutes. Remove roast to hot serving platter and garnish with pineapple slices. Pour roast juices into a saucepan; remove excess fat; heat and serve in sauce boat. Yield: 6 servings.

Note: A fresh pineapple may be used. Lay the strips of peel close together over the roast, just before roasting, in place of foil as directed above.

TOGO

Fish and Beef Sauce

- 1 pound beef, cut in 1-inch pieces
- 1 cup diced onion
- 3 tablespoons cooking oil, preferably peanut
- 1 teaspoon salt
- ¼ teaspoon pepper
- 2 cups water
- 1 pound shrimp, cooked and deveined
- 2 7-ounce cans crab meat
- 4 tomatoes, peeled and diced
- 1 teaspoon crushed red peppers
- 2 10-ounce packages frozen chopped spinach
- ¼ teaspoon ginger
- 2 tablespoons flour mixed with 2 tablespoons water
- 1 onion sliced

Cook beef and diced onions in fat in 12-inch frying pan over low heat for 15 minutes. Add salt, pepper, and water; simmer until meat is tender. To the meat, add the shrimp, crab, tomatoes and red pepper. Simmer for 15 minutes, stirring occasionally.

Cook spinach and drain well. Add spinach, ginger, flour paste, and onion to the meat mixture. Cover and cook over low heat for 10 minutes or until onion is tender; stir occasionally. Serve as entrée with rice. Yield: 6 servings.

TRINIDAD and TOBAGO

Almond-Chicken Arima

- ½ cup chopped onion
- ½ cup chopped cucumber
- ½ cup chopped carrots
- 1 8-ounce can water chestnuts, sliced
- 1 4-ounce can mushrooms, drained
- 1 8-ounce can bamboo shoots, drained
- 2 cups boiling water
- 2 cups diced raw chicken
- 3 tablespoons olive oil
- 1 teaspoon salt
- ¼ teaspoon monosodium glutamate
- ½ cup almonds or walnuts

Combine the first six ingredients in a bowl; pour water over the vegetables; cover and let stand 10 minutes. Uncover; drain.

Cook chicken over low heat in ⅔ of the olive oil for 15 to 20 minutes; add vegetables, salt, and monosodium glutamate. Blend and cook 5 minutes.

Cook almonds or walnuts in remaining oil until crisp and slightly brown.

Serve topped with nuts. Yield: 6 servings.

Note: For large scale recipe, divide chicken-vegetable mixture in 4 large roasting pans; cook covered in a 325°F oven for 20 minutes, stirring occasionally.

TUNISIA

Market-Zeïtun (Braised Beef and Olives)

- 1½ pounds round beef, cut in 1-inch cubes
- 2 tablespoons oil
- ½ cup water
- 1 1-pound can tomatoes
- 1 tablespoon minced parsley
- 1 clove garlic, minced
- ¼ teaspoon pepper
- 1 4½-ounce jar pitted green olives, sliced

Brown beef cubes in oil in 10-inch skillet; add water to loosen browned bits in pan. Combine tomatoes, parsley, garlic, and pepper; simmer for 5 minutes; add to meat and simmer for 1 hour. Add olives and continue to simmer for 30 minutes or until beef is tender. Sauce should be thick. Yield: 4-6 servings.

TURKEY

Baklava (Turkish Pastry)

Pastry:

2 cups flour
1 teaspoon salt
½ cup shortening
2 eggs, slightly beaten
2 tablespoons water

Filling:

1½ cups finely chopped walnuts or almonds
½ cup brown sugar, firmly packed
1 cup melted butter

Syrup:

1½ cups sugar
1 cup water
1 tablespoon lemon juice

Combine flour and salt. Cut shortening into flour until mixture is consistency of corn meal. Blend eggs and water; add to dry ingredients and mix until thoroughly dampened. Turn onto wax paper; knead lightly 6 to 8 times to make a smooth ball; let rest ½ hour. Divide pastry into 5 portions; roll each portion very thin on a lightly floured pastry cloth, into 8 x 8 inch squares. Place one square in bottom of 8-inch square pan.

To make filling: mix all ingredients together and divide into four portions. Spread ¼ of filling over pastry. Place second layer of pastry on top of filling. Spread with another ¼ of filling. Continue making layers until 4 portions of pastry and all of filling have been used. Place 5th portion of pastry on top. Cut Baklava into diagonal sections across the pan; then cut to form diamonds.

To make syrup: Combine syrup ingredients and boil for 5 minutes. Pour ½ of the syrup over Baklava. Bake in 350°F oven for 35 to 40 minutes. Serve remaining syrup, cooled, over warm Baklava. Yield: 9-12 servings.

Note: Turkish pastry or other rich pastry may be purchased in some frozen food departments; they may be used in place of pastry recipe given.

Kawerma (Lamb Hors d' Oeuvres)

1 pound chopped lamb
Water
½ teaspoon salt
1 tablespoon butter
1 tablespoon ground cumin

Form lamb in small balls about ¾-inch in diameter. Pour water, about 1-inch in depth, into large saucepan; add salt and bring to a boil. Drop the meat balls into boiling water to form single layer; reduce the heat; cover and simmer slowly until done. Remove meat balls; reduce liquid to ½ cup. Add butter and cumin to liquid; blend; and return meat balls to liquid. Cover and simmer for 10 to 15 minutes or until sauce has browned. Shake pan occasionally to cover balls with sauce and to avoid sticking. Serve as appetizers. Yield: 3 dozen small balls.

Salçali Köfte (Beef Balls in Tomato Sauce)

1½ pounds ground beef
1 large onion, grated
1 teaspoon chopped parsley
2½ slices dry whole wheat bread (soaked in water and squeezed dry)
2 eggs, slightly beaten
1 teaspoon salt
¼ teaspoon pepper
3 tablespoons flour
3 tablespoons butter
2 medium tomatoes, chopped, or ¼ cup tomato paste and 1 cup water

Combine meat, onion, parsley, bread, eggs, salt and pepper; mix thoroughly. Shape into balls the size of a walnut; dust with flour; brown in hot fat in large skillet. Add tomatoes or thinned paste to meat balls; simmer for 25 minutes. Serve hot as appetizers. Yield: 36 balls.

UGANDA

Plantains with Chicken Stew

2 pounds plantains or green bananas
Water
½ teaspoon salt
Few grains pepper

Chicken Stew:

1 3-pound frying chicken, cut for frying
¼ cup oil
1 large onion, sliced
2 tomatoes, peeled and cut in wedges or 1 cup canned tomatoes, drained
2 potatoes, peeled and sliced
1 teaspoon salt
½ teaspoon pepper
2 cups water

Peel the plantains or green bananas and place in a sauce pan with rack in the bottom. Add water, leaving the bananas above the level of the water. Add salt and pepper. Bring contents to boiling point; reduce heat and steam bananas until soft. Lift bananas from the liquid and mash well. Place in top of double boiler over simmering water until ready to serve with chicken stew.

To make Chicken Stew: fry chicken in hot oil in heavy frying pan or Dutch oven until brown. Add onions, tomatoes, potatoes, salt, pepper and water. Cover tightly and simmer about 1 hour or until chicken is tender.

Pour chicken stew over plantains. Yield: 6 servings.

Note: The plantain and the green banana (not the banana used generally by Americans in its green state) as prepared above tastes similar to mashed white potatoes.

UKRAINIAN SOVIET SOCIALIST REPUBLIC

Schnicel (Chicken Fillets à la Minister)

- 3 breasts of chicken, cut into halves and boned
- ½ cup flour
- ½ teaspoon salt
- 1 egg, beaten
- 1½ cups julienne strips or small cubes of fresh French bread
- 1 cup oil

Remove skin from chicken; split each breast half sufficiently so that fillet lies flat. Coat each fillet with flour; dip in salted egg mixture. Cover fillets with thin strips or small cubes of fresh French bread; press bread into egg mixture. Place breaded fillets in hot fat and brown quickly on both sides. Remove from fat; place on shallow baking sheet and cook in a 325°F oven for 15 minutes. Yield: 6 servings.

Varenyki (Cottage Cheese Ravioli)

- 2 cups flour
- ½ teaspoon salt
- 1 egg
- Water

Cheese Filling:

- ½ pound cottage cheese
- 2 tablespoons sour cream
- 2 eggs, beaten
- ¼ teaspoon salt
- 3 tablespoons sugar

- 1½ cups sour cream

Sift flour and salt into mixing bowl; make a depression in center, drop in egg and moisten with water to make a stiff dough. Knead until smooth; cover and let stand for 30 minutes. Divide dough in half and roll to ⅛-inch thickness. Cut into 2½ to 3-inch circles with cooky cutter.

To make Cheese Filling: mash cottage cheese with a fork; add sour cream, eggs, salt, and sugar. Mix well.

Place 1 heaping teaspoonful of cheese filling on lower half of circle; moisten edge of top half with water and fold. Press edges together firmly. Drop ravioli in large kettle, ¾ filled with boiling water. Cook for 5 to 7 minutes, counting time after water returns to boiling point. Serve as appetizer with sour cream. Yield: 12 servings.

UNION OF SOVIET SOCIALIST REPUBLICS

Health Salad

1 cucumber
1 carrot, peeled
1 apple
2 cups salad greens
2 teaspoons lemon juice
½ teaspoon salt
¼ cup sour cream
2 tomatoes, peeled

Cut the cucumber, carrot, and apple into thin or straw-like strips. Tear salad greens into easy-to-eat pieces. Place the greens and vegetable strips in a large bowl; add lemon juice and salt to vegetables and toss to mix well. Add sour cream and toss to coat all vegetables. Garnish with tomato wedges. Chill and serve. Yield: 6 servings.

Fried Fish Fritters

1½ pounds fish fillets, flounder, halibut
½ teaspoon salt
⅛ teaspoon pepper
2 tablespoons chopped parsley
Juice of 1 lemon
1 tablespoon salad oil

Fritter Batter:

1⅓ cups flour
½ teaspoon salt
2 teaspoons baking powder
⅔ cup milk
2 eggs, yolks and whites beaten separately
1 tablespoon oil

Fat for deep-fat frying

Cut fish in strips, 1-inch wide and 5 to 7-inches long. Salt and pepper fish and add parsley, lemon juice, and salad oil. Turn fillets to coat well and allow to marinate for 30 minutes.

To make fritter batter: sift flour, salt, and baking powder into mixing bowl; add milk, beaten egg yolks, and oil. Blend well; when ready to fry fish, fold beaten egg whites into batter.

Coat each fillet with fritter batter and fry in deep fat until brown. Serve fillets hot with tartar or hot tomato sauce. Yield: 6 servings.

Georgian Pheasant

- 1 2½-pound pheasant
- 1 teaspoon salt
- ¼ teaspoon pepper
- 6 thin slices salt pork
- 1 cup walnuts, coarsely chopped
- 1½ pounds white, seedless grapes, chopped
- 1 cup orange juice
- ½ cup Muscat wine
- ½ cup strong green tea
- ¼ cup flour, browned in oven
- ¼ cup butter

Rub inside of pheasant with salt and pepper. Skewer thin slices of salt pork over breast of pheasant; place in a 2½-quart casserole. Add walnuts, grapes, orange juice, wine and tea to pheasant; cover and bake for 1½ hours in a 350°F oven. When done, remove pheasant from casserole and place in shallow baking pan; remove salt pork and return pheasant to oven for 10 minutes of browning. To make sauce, mix flour and butter to a smooth paste; stir in ¼ cup of liquid in which pheasant was cooked. Blend and add to remaining broth in casserole. Cook and stir until sauce is thickened. Serve sauce with pheasant. Yield: 4-6 servings.

Okroshka Soup (Cold Russian Cream Soup)

- ½ pound boiled beef, ham, or tongue or combination
- 2 cucumbers, peeled and sliced thin
- 1 dozen green onions, chopped and mixed with ½ teaspoon salt
- 2 eggs, hard-cooked
- ½ cup sour cream
- 1 teaspoon sugar
- ¼ teaspoon prepared mustard
- ½ teaspoon salt
- 1 quart Kvas or dry ginger ale
- ½ cup chopped fennel

Kvas:

- 2 tablespoons pulverized rye bread crumbs
- 2 tablespoons sugar
- 3 raisins
- 1 pint water
- ½ teaspoon yeast

Cut boiled meat in small thin strips; combine meat, sliced cucumbers, chopped onions, and chopped whites of eggs.

Combine mashed egg yolks with sour cream, sugar, mustard, and salt.

To make Kvas: combine crumbs, sugar, raisins, and water; bring to boiling point and cool. Add sufficient water to make 1 quart; add yeast. Allow mixture to ferment for 1 or 2 days. When fermented, bottle and cap until used. (Yield: 1 quart.)

Add Kvas or ginger ale to egg yolk mixture and blend well. Add meat mixture to Kvas mixture; blend and chill thoroughly before serving. Garnish with fennel. Yield: 6 to 8 servings.

Baked Fish à la Moscow

- 6 fillets of fish, each weighing 6 to 8 ounces
- ½ teaspoon salt
- ¼ teaspoon pepper
- ½ cup flour
- ½ cup oil
- 2 cups Bechamel Sauce (page 102)
- ½ cup chopped onions, sautéed
- ½ cup sliced mushrooms, sautéed
- 1 cup cooked crab or lobster meat, flaked
- 3 hard-cooked eggs, quartered
- 3 medium potatoes, sliced and fried
- ¼ cup grated cheese

Coat each fillet with mixture of salt, pepper, and flour; fry in hot oil until both sides are brown. Place fillets in a baking dish, about 9 by 14 inches, over which a thin layer of Bechamel sauce has been spread. Add to the fillets, the onions, mushrooms, fish flakes, and eggs. Cover with fried potato slices. Pour remaining sauce on top of potatoes and sprinkle with cheese. Cook in a 350°F oven for 15 to 20 minutes or until thoroughly heated. Yield: 6 servings.

UNITED ARAB REPUBLIC

Cornish Game Hen Kolbasti

- 3 Cornish Game Hens, halved
- 1 teaspoon salt
- ¼ teaspoon pepper
- 2 tablespoons lemon juice
- 2 tablespoons onion juice
- 3 tablespoons butter
- 1 cup water

Pound each half Cornish Game Hen flat with meat mallet. Brush hens with mixture of salt, pepper, lemon and onion juices. Let stand for 15 minutes or longer. Place hens in hot butter in heavy skillet; cover and cook until brown. Turn hens; cover and brown other side. When brown, add water and continue cooking until hens are done. Serve with natural sauce or sauce thickened with browned flour. Yield: 6 servings.

Eggah (Egyptian Lamb Omelet)

- 1½ cups chopped lamb, cooked
- 1 medium onion, minced
- 4 tablespoons vegetable oil
- 2 tablespoons flour
- 6 large eggs, beaten
- 1 small clove garlic, minced
- 1 teaspoon cumin
- ⅛ teaspoon pepper
- 2 tablespoons parsley, chopped fine
- ¾ teaspoon salt

Cook lamb and onion in 2 tablespoons of oil until browned; mix the flour into the lamb and onion mixture and set aside.

Mix beaten eggs, garlic, cumin, pepper, parsley, and salt. Add onion and meat mixture; pour into skillet in which the other 2 tablespoons of oil have been heated. If electric frying pan is used, turn heat to 300°F; or cook over low heat. When the mixture will no longer flow, increase heat for a few seconds to brown the bottom. To turn omelet, place a plate over the omelet and turn omelet on the plate; return to skillet to finish cooking and browning. Yield: 6 servings.

Tagin Orz (Baked Rice with Chicken Livers)

- 1 large onion, thinly sliced
- 2 tablespoons butter
- ½ pound chicken livers, rinsed with cold water and dried
- ⅛ teaspoon pepper
- 1½ cups rice
- 2 cups chicken broth or 2 chicken bouillon cubes and 2 cups water
- ½ teaspoon salt

Cook onion in 1 tablespoon butter in frying pan until onions are golden brown. Remove onions and save; place livers in saucepan; add pepper and cook slowly until livers are brown. Place onions and livers in a 2-quart buttered casserole.

In same frying pan, cook rice in remaining tablespoon of butter, until rice is slightly brown. Add chicken broth and salt to rice and boil for 5 minutes. Mix rice with liver mixture in casserole; cover and bake for 20 minutes in 325°F oven. Remove cover and brown slightly. Yield: 6-8 servings.

UNITED KINGDOM OF GREAT BRITAIN AND NORTHERN IRELAND

Old English Christmas Fruit Cake

- 1 11-ounce package dried currants
- ½ pound dark seedless raisins
- ½ pound light seedless raisins
- 6½ ounces candied cherries, diced
- 2 ounces candied citron, diced
- 2 ounces candied orange peel, diced
- 4 ounces walnuts, ground
- 4 ounces blanched almonds, ground
- 1 cup brandy
- ½ pound butter or margarine
- ½ pound dark brown sugar
- 3 eggs, beaten
- 2 tablespoons dark molasses
- 1 teaspoon vanilla
- 1½ teaspoons glycerine
- 1½ teaspoons rose water
- 3 cups flour
- ½ teaspoon soda
- 1 teaspoon cinnamon
- ¼ teaspoon ginger, powdered
- ¼ teaspoon cloves, powdered

Mix fruits and nuts in a large bowl, at least 5-quart size, and soak in brandy overnight, covered.

Cream butter and sugar together; add eggs and beat very well. Add molasses, vanilla, glycerine and rose water and mix thoroughly.

Sift flour, soda and spices together twice. Add to the fruit and nut mixture and stir well. Add egg mixture to fruit and flour mixture. Mix well. Pour mixture into 10-inch spring form lined with a double layer of wax paper. Spread evenly. If smaller cake pans are used; fill ¾ full and bake shorter length of time. Bake 250°F for 1½ hours or until firm to touch. Cool slightly and remove from tin. Do not remove wax paper. Cool completely. Wrap in wax paper and seal in tins or plastic bags. Store for at least six weeks to season. Before serving, remove wax papers and slice thinly with very sharp knife. These cakes will last up to a year if properly sealed. Do not store in refrigerator. Yield: 1 10-inch cake.

Apricot Cobbler

- 1½ cups dried apricots
- Water
- 1 cup water
- 2 eggs, well beaten
- ¾ cup sugar
- ¾ cup flour
- 1½ teaspoon baking powder
- 6 tablespoons milk
- 1 teaspoon vanilla
- 3 tablespoons butter, melted
- Whipped cream

Wash apricots in cold water; cook with 1 cup water for 15 minutes. Combine eggs and sugar; beat until light and lemon colored. Sift flour and baking powder; add alternately with milk to egg and sugar mixture. Blend thoroughly; add vanilla and melted butter to batter.

Pour apricots into a 1½-quart buttered casserole; cover apricots with batter and bake for 30 to 40 minutes or until brown in a 350°F oven. Serve warm with whipped cream as a dessert. Yield: 6 servings.

Lemon Cheese Tarts

- 3 eggs
- 2 tablespoons grated lemon rind
- 6 tablespoons lemon juice
- ⅛ teaspoon salt
- ¾ cup sugar
- ¾ cup soft butter
- 8 tart shells, baked

Beat eggs in top of double boiler until light colored and well blended; stir in all of the other ingredients. Cook over hot water in the double boiler, stirring frequently, until mixture coats silver spoon and is thick, about 10 minutes.

Chill for 30 minutes or more; pour into prebaked individual tart shells, about 2-inches in diameter and rather shallow. Serve plain or with whipped cream. Yield: 6-8 tarts.

Tea Scones

- 4 cups flour
- 2 tablespoons baking powder
- 1 teaspoon salt
- ½ cup sugar
- ½ cup butter
- 1 medium egg, beaten
- 1 cup milk
- 2 tablespoons melted butter
- 2 tablespoons sugar

Sift flour, baking powder, salt, and sugar into a mixing bowl. Cut butter into the flour mixture until mixture is the consistency of corn meal. Combine egg and milk; add to flour mixture. Knead lightly on floured pastry cloth; roll out to ½-inch thickness. Cut into desired shape; brush scones with melted butter and sprinkle with sugar. Place on a greased cooky sheet and bake in 425°F oven for 15 minutes. Serve hot with butter and jam for tea or for breakfast. Yield: 20 or more scones, depending on size.

Lancashire Hot-Pot

1 pound lean, tender beef
5 medium potatoes
2 medium onions
2 medium carrots
2 ribs celery
1 teaspoon salt
½ teaspoon pepper
2 tablespoons chopped parsley
½ teaspoon mixed herbs
1 pint stock (canned bouillon or beef cubes may be used)

Cut the meat and vegetables into very thin slices. Place a layer of potatoes on the bottom of a 2-quart greased casserole; add a layer of meat, onions, carrots, and celery. Sprinkle some of each seasoning on each layer. Repeat order of potatoes, meat, onions, carrots, and celery. Top layer should be potatoes. Pour stock in casserole until ¾ full. Cover casserole and bake in 350°F oven for about 2 hours. Remove cover during last 30 minutes to brown potatoes. Yield: 6 servings.

Christmas Pudding

1½ cups currants
1 cup raisins
¼ cup chopped fruit peels
¼ cup coarsely chopped almonds
¾ cup finely chopped apples
1 cup chopped suet
½ cup flour
¼ teaspoon salt
1 teaspoon nutmeg
¾ cup sugar
1¾ cups soft breadcrumbs
2 egg yolks
1 egg white
1 teaspoon almond extract
1 teaspoon lemon juice
1 teaspoon grated lemon rind
2 tablespoons brandy

Combine currants, raisins, fruit peels, almonds, apple, and suet. Mix flour, salt, nutmeg, sugar, and breadcrumbs. Beat the egg yolks and white until light and add to flour mixture; stir in fruit mixture. Add extract, lemon juice, rind, and brandy.

Fill one medium and two small well-oiled pudding molds or tins ⅔ full of mixture. Cover each mold or tin with grease-proof paper and then cover with several layers of cheesecloth. Tie paper and cloth securely. Place molds in saucepan of boiling water; cover and steam 3 to 3½ hours. Add water as needed. Let cool. Puddings are best when allowed to ripen for about 2 months. Store in cool place. To serve, steam again for an hour; turn out on serving plate; pour slightly warmed brandy over the pudding; light with a match and serve with brandy butter. Yield: 2½ pounds or 12 servings.

UNITED REPUBLIC OF TANZANIA

Ndizi Na Nyama (Banana Medley)

- 8 bananas, peeled and cut in circles
- 1 cup onions, chopped
- 2 medium tomatoes, cubed
- 1 cup coconut milk (page 27)
- 1 tablespoon butter
- ½ teaspoon salt
- ¼ teaspoon turmeric

Combine all ingredients listed in a 2-quart saucepan. Bring to a boil; reduce heat and simmer for 15 minutes. Serve with beef. Yield: 6-8 servings.

Red Bean Soup

- 2 cups red beans
- Boiling water
- 2 pounds beef soup bones
- 2 large onions, chopped
- 2 tablespoons fat
- 2 tomatoes, cut in small pieces
- 1 tablespoon flour
- 1 teaspoon salt

Wash beans; cover with 2 or 3 times as much boiling water as beans; boil 2 minutes; remove from heat and soak 1 hour or more. Simmer beans and beef bones in same water until tender or about 1 hour. Remove the bones and mash the beans. Sauté the onions in fat until tender; add tomatoes and flour. Stir and cook over low heat until color changes to golden brown. Add onion mixture to mashed beans; add salt, bones, and more water, if necessary. Simmer for 30 minutes. Remove the bones and serve as is or strain the soup. Serve very hot. Yield: 6-8 servings.

UNITED STATES OF AMERICA

Roast Turkey with Chestnut-Sausage Dressing

1 10 to 12-pound turkey hen
Salt

Prepare turkey for roasting. Sprinkle inside of cleaned, dry turkey with salt. (Save giblets and neck to make a broth for the gravy.)

Dressing:

1 pound chestnuts
2 cups day-old bread, cubed
1½ cups to 2 cups milk
3 green onions, chopped
1 cup celery, diced
2 tablespoons butter
1 pound pork sausage bulk

To make Chestnut-Sausage Dressing: peel the chestnuts by making a slit in each shell with a pointed knife. Bake the nuts in a 400°F oven for 15 minutes or boil for the same length of time in water to cover, then drain. When nuts are cool remove shells and inner skins. Put through food mill using fine blade or chop finely. Soak bread in milk. Cook onions and celery in butter until transparent but not brown. Add sausage meat to onions and celery mixture; combine well and cook over low heat until sausage is slightly browned. Combine bread, chestnuts, and sausage mixture.

1 stick butter or margarine

Stuff turkey with this mixture. Use poultry pins or short skewers to keep opening closed, lacing the skewers with twine to make secure. Press thighs of the bird close to the body; tie with twine.

Rub the outside of the bird with soft melted butter or margarine; place, breast side up, on the rack in a shallow pan. Cover loosely with aluminum foil; roast in a 350°F oven for 5 to 5½ hours. Remove foil during last 30 minutes for bird to brown. Keep bird warm while making a pan gravy, using broth in which giblets and neck were simmered. Yield: 12 to 15 servings.

Note: Dressing can be baked in covered casserole and served with turkey.

Eggplant Casserole

- 1 large chopped onion
- 3 tablespoons butter
- 2 small eggplants, peeled and diced
- 1 28-ounce can tomatoes, drained
- 1 teaspoon salt
- ½ teaspoon black pepper
- ¼ cup corn flake crumbs, buttered
- Parsley

Sauté onions in 1 tablespoon melted butter until golden; remove from pan. Sauté eggplants in same pan with 2 tablespoons melted butter until golden brown. Add sautéed onions, tomatoes, salt and pepper and mix thoroughly. Pour into casserole, top with corn flake crumbs. Bake at 325°F for 30 minutes. Serve hot garnished with parsley. Yield: 6 servings.

Seafood Chowder

- 2 ribs celery, chopped
- 1 cup onion, finely chopped
- 3 tablespoons butter, melted
- 2½ cups potatoes, diced
- 3 cups water
- 1 6-ounce can crabmeat
- 1 5½-ounce can shrimp
- 1 teaspoon salt
- ¼ teaspoon pepper
- 1 cup American cheese, grated
- 1 quart milk
- Parsley

Cook celery and onion in melted butter until tender. Do not brown. Add potatoes and water; cook 15 minutes or until potatoes are tender. Do not overcook. Add remaining ingredients, except the parsley, to mixture.

Heat slowly until cheese melts and mixture is thoroughly heated. Do not boil. Serve hot; garnish with parsley. Yield: 6 servings.

Note: May be refrigerated and reheated. Do not boil when reheating. Flavor improves on standing.

Spiced Hot Fruit

- 1 29-ounce can Elberta peach halves, drained
- 1 29-ounce can apricot halves, drained
- 3 apples, peeled, cored, and cut in ½-inch slices
- 2 cups fresh or frozen strawberries
- 2 firm bananas, sliced lengthwise
- ½ cup Cointreau or Grand Marnier
- ½ cup honey
- ½ cup brown sugar
- 2 teaspoons cinnamon
- 1 teaspoon nutmeg
- 1 cup walnut halves, unsalted

Place all fruit, except the bananas in a 2-quart casserole; pour liqueur and honey over the fruit; sprinkle with sugar and spices. Cover casserole until time for baking.

Bake uncovered in a 400°F oven for 20 minutes. Remove casserole from the oven; cover fruit with banana slices and sprinkle with nuts. Return to oven and bake for 10 minutes. Serve hot as dessert. Yield: 8 to 10 servings.

Veal Sauté

- 2 pounds boneless veal, cut in strips 2″ x 1″
- ½ cup flour
- 2 tablespoons cooking oil
- 2 medium onions, finely chopped
- 1 3½-ounce can sliced mushrooms, drained
- ¼ teaspoon powdered thyme
- ¼ teaspoon powdered garlic
- 2 tablespoons Worcestershire sauce
- ¼ teaspoon black pepper
- 1 cup chicken bouillon

Roll veal strips in flour; brown in oil, a few strips at a time, and remove from pan as strips brown. Keep meat warm. In same pan cook onions and mushrooms until onions are yellow. Add browned veal and all seasonings to onion and mushroom mixture. Combine well and add ½ cup bouillon. Simmer covered over low heat for 45 minutes, or until meat is tender. Add remaining bouillon as needed. Serve over fluffy white or saffron rice. Yield: 6 servings.

Shrimp-Avocado Salad

- 1½ pounds cooked shrimp, deveined and cut in half, lengthwise
- 1 cup diced celery
- 2 avocados, cut in 1-inch cubes
- 1 3½-ounce can pitted ripe olives, drained and sliced
- 6 ounces olives condite (olive salad), sliced

Salad Sauce:

- 1 cup mayonnaise
- ⅓ cup green pickle relish
- ⅓ cup chili sauce
- ⅓ cup French dressing
- 3 tablespoons minced green onions
- 1 teaspoon powdered oregano
- 1 teaspoon caraway seeds (optional)
- ½ teaspoon garlic powder

Combine salad ingredients just before serving.

To make salad sauce: combine all ingredients in a pint jar; shake well and refrigerate. (Sauce may be prepared days in advance.)

Add sauce to coat ingredients, tossing lightly. Yield: 6 main-course servings or 12 appetizers.

UPPER VOLTA

Maan Nezim Nzedo (Fish Stew with Vegetables)

- ½ cup vegetable oil
- 2 8-ounce cans tomato sauce
- 1 onion, sliced thin
- ¼ teaspoon red pepper
- 2 teaspoons salt
- 1½ pounds fresh water fish, catfish preferred
- 1 package frozen okra, pods cut in halves
- 3 carrots, cut in ¼-inch slices
- 1 small head cabbage, quartered and sliced
- 1 package frozen green beans
- 1 cup rice

Combine oil, tomato sauce, onion, pepper and salt in a 12-inch skillet and bring to a boil. Add to this mixture, the fish cut into 6 serving pieces, okra, carrots, cabbage, and beans; cover; bring mixture to a boil and cook over low heat for 5 minutes. Add rice and continue cooking for 25 minutes; add water during cooking, if necessary. Yield: 6 servings.

URUGUAY

Beefsteak Pie

- 1 medium onion, chopped
- 2 tablespoons oil
- 1 pound round beefsteak, chopped
- 1 cup raisins
- 3 hard-cooked eggs, chopped
- 1 teaspoon salt
- 1 teaspoon sugar
- 1 cup grated Cheddar cheese
- 2 cups mashed potatoes, well seasoned
- ½ cup dried breadcrumbs

Cook onion in hot oil until onion is yellow. Add meat to onions and brown meat lightly; add raisins, eggs, salt, sugar, and ½ cup cheese to meat and onion mixture. Put in a 2-quart oiled casserole; cover with mashed potatoes. Sprinkle remaining ½ cup cheese and breadcrumbs over potatoes. Bake for 20 minutes in a 350°F oven. Serve hot. Yield: 6 servings.

VENEZUELA

Spicy Chopped Meat Dish

- 1/4 cup butter or margarine
- 2 tablespoons olive oil
- 1/2 cup water
- 1 teaspoon salt
- 1/2 teaspoon black pepper
- 1 pound beef, chopped
- 1/2 to 1 teaspoon hot crushed red peppers
- 1/2 teaspoon tarragon
- 1/2 teaspoon oregano
- Juice of 1 orange
- 1/4 of orange rind, grated or chopped finely
- 2 onions, chopped
- 1/2 cup raisins, soaked in cold water
- 1/2 cup tomato catsup or chili sauce

Melt butter or margarine in a 10-inch frying pan; add olive oil, water, salt, and pepper. Bring to a boil; add ground beef; break with a fork. Cover and simmer slowly for 5 minutes, stirring occasionally. Add the crushed pepper, tarragon, oregano, and orange juice. Simmer for 5 minutes; stir meat to separate into small pieces. Add the orange rind, onions, raisins, and catsup. Simmer for 20 minutes, stirring occasionally. Add water if mixture becomes dry. Yield: 4 to 6 servings.

Chicken Pie

- 1/2 cup flour
- 2 cups chicken broth
- 2 cups canned tomatoes
- 2 onions, quartered and sliced
- 2 tablespoons red pimiento, diced
- 1 cup ripe olives, pitted
- 2 tablespoons capers
- 3 cups diced, cooked chicken (4 to 5 pound hen)

Crust:

- 2 cups flour
- 2 teaspoons sugar
- 1/2 cup shortening
- 1/4 cup butter
- 2 egg yolks, beaten
- 1/4 cup sweet wine

Mix flour with 1/2 cup cold broth; blend well to smooth paste. Add remaining broth and tomatoes; cook over low fire until mixture boils, stirring constantly. Add other ingredients, including chicken, and bring to a boil.

To make crust: blend the flour, sugar, shortening and butter together. Add egg yolks and wine; mix with a fork, handling lightly. Divide dough in half. Roll out both halves on a floured board and fit one in a 2-quart casserole.

Pour mixture into unbaked pie crust and cover with the remaining crust cut to fit top of casserole. Bake in a 425°F oven for 10 minutes. Reduce heat to 325°F and continue cooking for 30 minutes. Yield: 6-8 servings.

YEMEN

Malfoof Mahshie (Stuffed Cabbage)

- 1 medium head cabbage
- 1 cup rice
- 1 pound ground lamb or beef
- 1 teaspoon salt
- ¼ teaspoon pepper
- 1 clove of garlic, halved
- 2 cups canned tomatoes
- Juice of 1 lemon

Wash cabbage; cut away outer leaves, stem, and core. Boil in large kettle of water until cabbage is pliable or wilted. Separate each leaf with a fork; let leaves cool. Line the bottom of a 10 x 15 inch baking pan with outer leaves.

Cook rice according to package directions until almost tender; drain. Add meat, salt, and pepper.

Remove center stem of inner cabbage leaves; cut each leaf into 2 pieces; rub with the cut end of the clove of garlic. Place about 2 tablespoons of rice and meat mixture on each piece of cabbage leaf; roll leaf firmly around the mixture as if rolling a frankfurter; tuck ends under and place edge side down on cabbage leaves in baking pan.

Combine tomatoes and lemon juice; pour over cabbage rolls. Cover, foil may be used; bake in 350°F oven for 1 hour. Yield: 20-24 appetizers.

YUGOSLAVIA

Podvarak (Baked Sauerkraut)

¼ cup diced onion
3 tablespoons butter
¼ teaspoon pepper
3 small or short hot peppers, cut fine
¼ cup water
2 cups sauerkraut

Cook onion in butter until yellow; add pepper and hot peppers; simmer for 5 minutes. Add 1 or 2 tablespoons of water, if needed. Add sauerkraut and remaining water; cover and simmer for 20 minutes. Bake in a 300°F oven for 1 hour; add water, if needed. Yield: 4-6 servings.

Pikantne Šnicle (Savory Veal Cutlets)

2 pounds veal cutlets
4 tablespoons oil
1 cup chopped onion
Peel of 1 lemon, finely chopped
1 teaspoon lemon juice
1 egg yolk, beaten
1 pint sour cream
1 tablespoon prepared mustard
½ teaspoon salt

Pound the veal until thin and cut into 6 to 8 pieces. Brown both sides of veal quickly in hot oil. Remove from fat and keep hot.

Add onion to remaining fat and cook until transparent; add lemon peel and juice. Combine egg yolk, sour cream, mustard and salt with onion mixture. Place over low heat until mixture is hot, but not boiling. Pour sauce over cutlets. Yield: 6 servings.

Triglav Cream (Apple Cream)

3 eggs, separated
1¼ cups milk
½ cup plus 1½ tablespoons sugar
1 envelope or 1 tablespoon unflavored gelatin
1 apple, peeled and cut in tiny cubes
½ pint cream, whipped
1 pint whole strawberries

Beat egg yolks until foamy; add the milk, sugar, and gelatin; mix thoroughly; cook in double boiler until thick, stirring constantly. Cool. Beat egg whites until soft peaks form. Fold egg whites and apple cubes into milk mixture. Pour mixture into an oiled 1-quart mold and refrigerate. Small molds may be used. When cream is firmly set, unmold; serve with whipped cream and strawberries. Yield: 6 servings.

Large-Scale
Buffet Menus and Recipes
to Serve 50 Persons

DIPLOMATIC RECEPTION

ITALY

Funghi Ripieni

(Stuffed Mushrooms)

See page 70

100 large mushrooms, fresh
2 quarts bread crumbs
1 tablespoon salt
2 teaspoons pepper
1 cup parsley, finely chopped
8 cloves garlic, minced
1¼ quarts chicken bouillon
1 cup olive oil
1 quart white cooking wine

ALGERIA

Algerian Meat Balls

(160 Meat Balls)

See page 10

8 slices dry bread
2 cups milk
4 pounds ground beef or lamb
2 cups finely chopped onion
2 teaspoons dried dill weed
2 cups fresh parsley, or 1 cup dried parsley
2 teaspoons dried mint leaves
4 eggs, slightly beaten
1 tablespoon salt
1 teaspoon pepper
Oil or fat for deep fat frying

IRELAND

Queen Cakes

See page 66

2¼ cups margarine
3 cups superfine granulated sugar
9 large eggs, well beaten
9 cups flour, sifted
2 tablespoons baking powder
1 pint milk (add alternately with flour mixture)

TURKEY

Baklava

(Turkish Pastry)

See page 116

Pastry:

2½ quarts (2½ pounds) sifted flour
⅓ cup (5 ounces) salt
2½ cups (1 pound, 4 ounces) shortening
10 eggs, slightly beaten
⅔ cup water
(Use 12 x 18 x 2-inch pans)

Filling:

7½ cups (2 pounds) finely chopped walnuts or almonds
1 pound brown sugar
2 pounds butter, melted

Syrup:

3 pounds sugar
1 quart water
¼ cup lemon juice

UNITED KINGDOM

Tea Scones

See page 125

8 cups sifted flour
4 tablespoons baking powder
1 tablespoon salt
¾ cup sugar
½ pound butter or margarine
4 eggs, beaten
2 cups milk
¼ pound melted butter
6 tablespoons sugar

AFRICAN NIGHT

TUNISIA

Market-Zeïtun

(Braised Beef with Olives)

See page 115

14 pounds round of beef, cut in
1-inch cubes with
2 tablespoons salt
⅔ cup oil
3 cups water
5 28-ounce cans tomatoes
8 cloves garlic, crushed
2 teaspoons pepper
4 10-ounce jars pimiento stuffed
green olives
(Use 3-gallon pot)

LIBERIA

Jollof Rice

(Chicken and Meat with Rice)

See page 78

18 pounds frying chicken, cut into
serving pieces
1½ cups oil
3 pounds smoked ham, cut in 1-inch
cubes or 6 pounds lean spare ribs
12 medium onions (3 pounds), sliced
3 tablespoons salt
1½ teaspoons pepper
1 tablespoon ground allspice
2 No. 10 cans tomatoes
2¼ pints tomato paste
2¼ pints water
1½ pounds string beans, fresh
or frozen
6 cups raw rice
6 quarts salted water

SOUTH AFRICA

Yellow Peach Pickle

See page 107

4 30-ounce cans sliced peaches
2⅔ cups peach juice
1 quart vinegar
4 teaspoons peppercorns
4 teaspoons coriander seeds
4 teaspoons whole allspice
2 teaspoons salt
1⅓ cups brown sugar
4 teaspoons cornstarch
2 teaspoons turmeric
4 teaspoons curry powder
2 cups chopped onion
4 tablespoons chopped chili pepper
or 2 tablespoons crushed red
peppers

CHAD

Squash with Peanuts

See page 32

20 to 22½ pounds summer squash
or zucchini
Salt
Water
7 cups shelled, roasted peanuts
¾ cup fat
3 tablespoons sugar, optional

DAHOMEY

Wonders Dessert

See page 42

3½ quarts sifted flour
8 teaspoons salt
3 cups butter
2 cups water
½ cup vegetable oil
Fat for frying
4 cups sugar
4 teaspoons cinnamon or mace

LATIN AMERICAN FIESTA

COSTA RICA

Mousse de Aguacate
(Avocado Mousse)

See page 38

8 large avocados, peeled, seeded, cut in small pieces
¼ cup grated onion
4 teaspoons salt
2 teaspoons Worcestershire Sauce
3 tablespoons (3 pkgs.) unflavored gelatin
3 cups cold water
1 cup boiling water
2 cups whipped cream
2 cups mayonnaise

PERU

Arroz Jimeno
(Veal and Pork with Rice)

See page 98

100 thin slices of veal steak (about 11 pounds)
50 thin slices of pork steak (about 14 pounds)
2½ tablespoons salt
2 teaspoons pepper
2 cups flour
3 cups vegetable oil
1 quart sherry
1 quart water
½ cup cornstarch mixed with 2 cups water
1 quart onions, diced
1½ quarts green peppers, diced
1 quart red peppers, diced
8 cloves garlic, minced
1 cup butter
5 quarts cooked rice
1 cup raisins
1 cup sliced almonds
16 hard-cooked eggs, chopped
4 cups cooked peas
½ cup minced parsley

ECUADOR

Seviche (Pickled Fish)

See page 45

9 pounds thin fillets of bass or any delicate fish
4½ cups lemon juice
2 cups orange juice
¾ cup tomato catsup
6 medium onions, chopped
6 chili peppers, minced
6 sweet red peppers, chopped
6 sweet green peppers, chopped
1½ cups corn kernels
4½ teaspoons salt

TRINIDAD AND TOBAGO

Almond-Chicken Arima

See page 115

1 quart chopped onions
1 quart chopped cucumbers
1 quart thinly sliced carrots
3 pounds canned water chestnuts, washed, drained, sliced thinly
2 pounds canned, sliced mushrooms, drained
4 pounds canned, sliced bamboo shoots, drained
1 gallon boiling water
5 quarts diced raw chicken
1½ cups olive oil
1 tablespoon salt
1 tablespoon monosodium glutamate
1 quart split almonds or walnuts

ARGENTINA

Sopa de Manzanas
(Apple Sauce)

See page 12

15 pounds green apples, cut in eighths
Water
Peel of 2 lemons
5 cups sugar
2½ cups raisin, soaked in warm water
10 egg yolks, slightly beaten

FAR EAST BUFFET

MALAYSIA

Sambal-Goreng

(Shrimp with Green Pepper)

See page 83

8 medium (2½ pounds) onions, cut fine
24 green onions including tops, cut fine
2 cups vegetable oil
8 green bell peppers, cut in thin strips
24 (11 pounds) tomatoes, peeled and cubed
4 cups blanched almonds, slivered
4 pounds fresh shrimp, cleaned and deveined
4 teaspoons basil
4 teaspoons thyme
8 teaspoons salt
2 teaspoons white pepper
1 cup flour
6 cups coconut milk (page 27)
(Use 20 quart kettle)

PHILIPPINES

Asado de Carajay

(Pork Paprika)

See page 100

14 pounds boneless pork shoulder butt, sliced in long slices
1 tablespoon pepper
¼ cup salt
8 cloves garlic, crushed
½ cup oil
8 bay leaves
2 cups vinegar
½ cup paprika
1½ quarts water
32 medium onions, quartered
1 28-ounce can tomatoes
(Use 3-gallon pot)

CEYLON

Deviled Fish

See page 31

10 large onions, chopped
¼ cup oil
½ cup dry mustard
⅓ cup chili powder
8 bay leaves
3 tablespoons salt
½ cup Worcestershire sauce
⅓ cup sugar
2 quarts light cream or coconut milk
1 cup vinegar
14 pounds fresh or frozen fish

CHINA

3-Cup Chicken

See page 34

1½ quarts sherry
3 cups soy sauce
3⅓ cups oil
8 quarts boned, cut-up chicken or 8 4-pound chickens
3½ quarts chopped onions
30 cloves garlic, minced
¼ cup powdered ginger
¼ cup sugar
Cornstarch, if needed to thicken sauce.

MALAYSIA

Inti-puff

(Coconut Surprise)

See page 83

1 cup plus 2 tablespoons dark brown sugar, packed
1 cup plus 2 tablespoons granulated sugar
5½ tablespoons cornstarch
1 cup water, cold
3 4-ounce cans flaked coconut
Plain pastry, 3 recipes
3 medium eggs, beaten

5 CONTINENTS DINNER

ITALY

Involtini

(Rolled Veal with Pâté)

See page 70

16 pounds veal cutlets, cut very thin
2 tablespoons ground rosemary
3 cups flour
1 pound grated Parmesan cheese
3 tablespoons salt
2 teaspoons pepper
8 4-ounce cans pâté de foie gras
½ pound butter
½ cup chopped parsley
1 cup oil
2 quarts Marsala or dry white wine

INDIA

Benegal Fish Curry

See page 62

16 dried chili peppers, finely crushed
3 tablespoons turmeric
3 tablespoons salt
16 pounds halibut steak, cut in 1-inch cubes
¾ cup vegetable oil

Curry Sauce:

2½ tablespoons coriander seeds
2½ tablespoons cardamon seeds
2 tablespoons cumin seeds
5 tablespoons mustard seeds
14 pounds onions
2½ tablespoons turmeric
1½ tablespoons cinnamon
2 teaspoons chili powder
2 tablespoons salt
25 to 30 cloves garlic
2 cups vegetable oil
8 pounds tomatoes, peeled and sliced
2 quarts yogurt

UNITED STATES OF AMERICA

3 Roast Turkeys with Chestnut-Sausage Dressing

See page 128

SUDAN

Shorbat Robe

(Yogurt and Cucumber Salad)

See page 110

10 large cucumbers, pared and chopped
5 pints yogurt
1 tablespoon salt
¾ teaspoon garlic powder
¾ teaspoon ground black pepper

PERU

Leche Asada

(Custard with Cognac)

See page 99

8 14½-ounce cans evaporated milk
2⅔ cups water
1 pint cognac
2 cups sugar
24 eggs, slightly beaten
1 teaspoon cinnamon
1 teaspoon nutmeg

INDEX

Appetizers

Soups

Main Dishes — Fish

Main Dishes — Meat

Main Dishes – Poultry

Casseroles

Vegetables

Salads, Relishes, and Sauces

Desserts

Miscellaneous

Large – Scale Buffet Menus and Recipes: